Blossom Like Eden is a
rest and fullness of freed...
testimony is clothed with gentle humility and transformative truth. *Blossom Like Eden* will lead you to your own Deep Place with God, and it profoundly impacted my faith journey. Her reflection questions at the end of each chapter led me to discover the same truths she wrote. She uncovered truths that many of us have known our whole lives yet somehow failed to really understand and live out. While reading, I felt as if I had my own personal spiritual sister-mentor guiding me on the path to freedom in Christ. What a gift this book is, and it shall be a go-to for any young woman I mentor in the future.

—Svea Braun, Minister, Teacher, Christian Speaker, and Mentor

Not your standard book on "how to grow as a Christian," *Blossom Like Eden* points out clear ways in which God shows up in our everyday lives that we can easily overlook. I was stirred to slow my pace and anticipate His presence, His voice, and His guiding hand. I suddenly noticed too that He had spoken into my life in the past and I hadn't even realized it. Some books are so riveting you just can't put them down; however, this book entices me to stop repeatedly in eagerness to talk to Jesus and experience Him too.

—Monique Desorcy, Children's Ministry Coordinator, Southland Church

A beautiful journey from start to finish, Sarah gently nudges the reader towards a deeper, more intimate place with the Father. *Blossom Like Eden* will inspire you to take your next step towards fullness and freedom in Christ.

—Joanna Froese, Pastor, New City Church

Over the years, I have watched Sarah live out the story she shares in these pages. With obedience and trust, she has followed God's gentle leading into places of surrender and healing. Because of her willingness to step out in faith and welcome Him into the deep, sometimes painful, places in her life, she has come out changed, shining with a light that shows others a path through their own hard places. Her words are an offering of hope and a witness to the goodness and faithfulness of God when we surrender and allow Him to breathe new life into places we didn't think could bloom again.

—Kendra Dueck, Christian Speaker and Writer

In *Blossom Like Eden*, Sarah shares her story of how God led her into fullness of life, and in the process, we experience God's gentle beckoning to take this same journey ourselves. This book is for everybody who feels like a nobody. With a voice of truth totally devoid of condemnation, Sarah will help you to see yourself as the Daughter of the King you truly are.

—Stephanie Armbruster, YWAM Bible Teacher,
Master of Arts in Biblical Languages and Educational Ministries

Blossom like Eden

Blossom like Eden

Come out of Hiding
and into the Son

Sarah Brandt

BLOSSOM LIKE EDEN
Copyright © 2020 by Sarah Brandt

Printed in Canada

ISBN: 978-1-4866-1946-7
eBook ISBN: 978-1-4866-1947-4

Word Alive Press
119 De Baets Street Winnipeg, MB R2J 3R9
www.wordalivepress.ca

Cataloguing in Publication information can be obtained from Library and Archives Canada.

For my daughters,
Cadence, Lexis, and Scarlett:
Just bloom …

The Lord will comfort Israel again and have pity on her ruins.
Her desert will blossom like Eden,
her barren wilderness like the garden of the Lord.
Joy and gladness will be found there.
Songs of thanksgiving will fill the air.
(Isaiah 51:3)

Preface

A NEW LEAF

*"But the godly will flourish like palm trees
and grow strong like the cedars of Lebanon"*
(Psalm 92:12).

A tender shoot. A new leaf. It was the picture God gave me right before I was taken into the journey of the fullness of life. It was like the picture from Isaiah, where God cuts down the tree to a stump, and out of the stump grows a tender new shoot of life, a leaf. From what looked old and useless comes this vibrant burst of colour, just like our lives in Him. The old is cut away as we enter into our new life in Him. That stump represented much more than just my old life. It represented the way I was believing in God and living out my faith. God had to cut it all away before I could turn over a new leaf, change my way of living, and begin a new existence in Him. I'd spent so much time living for Him instead of with Him. I'd spent years looking at other women of faith and wondering what they had that I didn't. Something inside of them was alive, and their joy overflowed, while I struggled to remember to pray every day and fit my devotions in where I could. It wasn't easy to keep it up—the feeling of connection with Him. I had to work at it. I had to fit it in. I was close to Him some days, and then at times I felt so far away.

Throughout the Bible, God uses a specific picture of Himself. He begins with a beautiful garden called Eden. Imagine it, with its balmy temperatures and lush, green vegetation. Every plant thrives; no weeds choke them out. The flowers are budding and the apple trees have blossoms. It's a living masterpiece, a small piece of Heaven on Earth. The garden enjoys pristine conditions in order to keep the greenery growing and in peak condition. Our Master, God Himself, is the gardener, the landscape artist behind the scene. He has carefully planned where each plant will grow and every element in the soil. He has perfected a garden aesthetically pleasing and organic, choosing humankind to live inside its beauty.

In our humanness, we resist the easy comfort with our "What if?" questions and self-doubt, ruining this picturesque garden and leaving only wilderness. Human after human wanders inside their own wilderness of power-hunger and identity-doubt. The Old Testament is full of stories in which God needs to come in and redeem and re-grow each people group. Finally, the book of Isaiah begins to paint a picture of hope, something that will change this overgrowth of sin back to its original state. A Saviour. He's called a tender shoot from the stump of Israel. He will come to bring new life like we haven't seen since the garden. He promises the fullness of life through His death, and the restoration of the relational faith that was broken with the fall of man.

The New Testament begins with the story of this new shoot, Jesus. He comes and lives a restful pace of life here on Earth, bringing glory to His Father's name and telling stories of scattering seeds, enjoying new life, pruning away the old, and making room for the new to survive. The Saviour dies, and with His resurrection, He invites us to walk out of the grave with Him, re-born. The new kingdom family begins to grow. The rest of the New Testament speaks of promises for each new member of His family—promises for good and not for harm. Promises to heal and comfort. Promises that one day we will be fully glorified, flourishing again, like in the Garden of Eden. It's a full-circle story of redemption. From beauty, to ashes, to beauty again. A love so great that He faced the cross so humankind could have another chance to see God for who He is and how much He cares.

God wants us to flourish like Eden. He invites us to accept every promise He offers in His Word, yet we settle for a life like the wandering Israelites. Removed from God, living like strangers to His work, we continue to seek esteem, accomplishments, and reward instead of the free gift He has placed in front of us. We look to outside influences to measure our self-worth, and we wallow in false humility. We have a scale to judge achievement, and a bitter obsession with comparison. This is where we live—right in the thick of it without much vision to see past the tangle of weeds right in front of us.

God says that there is more to life than wandering. He knows exactly who you are and what you're carrying, and He offers to teach you the way to live in the fullness of life He has gifted you. He desires for you to be a garden that He tends. He says that He is our friend, our Father, our healer. These are the places He took me. The journey to fullness is about connecting with His heart for you. Each chapter of this book reveals a gift within that fullness as I recount my experiences wandering in the wilderness and how He untangled the weeds to bear fruit again. It was the plan God had from the beginning, to make a way for us to live blossoming in Him, a taste of Heaven here on Earth until He comes back for us. He is beckoning you now; take His hand and walk with Him out of the desert and into the garden again.

"For from his fullness we have all received, grace upon grace"
(John 1:16, ESV).

Chapter One

THE FULLNESS OF INTIMACY
—Falling in Love with Your Saviour

It was a standoff. Me against the black, woven book on the shelf. I could see it staring at me like in an old Western movie, where the bad guy and the good guy stand face-to-face, and you don't know who's going to draw their gun first. The Bible, I suppose, was the good guy. Did that make me the crook? The usual condemnation and guilt were washing over me. *I should pick it up and read it already! What's stopping me? There's so much I need to get done today. The dishes aren't going to rinse themselves, and that frying pan has been in the sink since last night. I have to teach the girls school, and then there's that promise to pick up donations for the ministry this afternoon.* Laying down arms, I said a quick apology in my head and fled the scene, the promise to come back later left in the dust of avoidance.

I wanted to want to read it. I'd seen those women who were immersed in the Bible. I could tell that their joy came with ease, and their answers to my hard questions produced an impactful air of gentleness. They held a certain position in Christ, that much was obvious. They acted like they knew Him—not as a God, but something deeper, something rooted. It felt lonely sometimes on the sidelines of those women. Something wasn't clicking for me like it was for them. What was I doing so differently from them?

Sermon after sermon, book after book taught me the importance of staying in the Word. "Staying in the Word"—what sort of phrase was that? "Staying" meant all sorts of things: rest, continuance, lingering. How was someone supposed to linger in God's Word, with its hard-to-pronounce kings' names, not to mention the endless lists of genealogy? I wasn't a Bible scholar, so I didn't understand all the nuances, or why those last names held so much status. It would take me years to figure it out, so I believed it was safest to stay in the Psalms or Ephesians. Those were the good chapters that spoke on love and how much He takes care of us.

When I began my new life as a Christian, I found security. It was a protection that my world had never offered me and that my soul craved. I began to learn about God's love for me, and slowly my life changed. Many years went by. I was married, had children, and was living a steady, stable life. It was the type of life many Christians live. I thought I loved God. I'd accepted Him as my Saviour, I believed the Bible was true, and I tried my best to go to church every Sunday and live as the best version of myself I could be. I was serving in a ministry that helped the poor and immersing myself in Bible studies, sermons, podcasts, and beautiful books on freedom in Christ and living your best life. I was so busy raising my family and leading my ministry that I fit my Bible times in here and there, comforting myself with the idea that most of my friends didn't have a set devotional time either. Besides, the main point was that Jesus died, right? I was saved and would go to Heaven one day to be with Him. If I understood that, then I felt that the rest would fall into place.

One day a passage in Ephesians caught my attention and confirmed in my heart that I wasn't understanding a key truth. Though my life looked stable, and my Christian walk seemed normal, I felt something deeper beckoning. Paul writes:

> *When I think of all this, I fall to my knees and pray to the Father, the*
> *Creator of everything in heaven and on earth. I pray that from*

his glorious, unlimited resources he will empower you with inner strength through his Spirit. Then Christ will make his home in your hearts as you trust in him. Your roots will grow down into God's love and keep you strong. And may you have the power to understand, as all God's people should, how wide, how long, how high, and how deep his love is. May you experience the love of Christ, though it is too great to understand fully. Then you will be made complete with all the fullness of life and power that comes from God. Now all glory to God, who is able, through his mighty power at work within us, to accomplish infinitely more than we might ask or think. Glory to him in the church and in Christ Jesus through all generations forever and ever! Amen. (Ephesians 3:14–21, emphasis added)

This passage didn't reflect what I was living. I felt like God was up higher, a king that looked down on me. I was convinced that the way to gain access to Him was through prayer. Christianity meant believing He'd died for me, serving Him, and giving a tithe faithfully to the church. But these verses said something different. They spoke of a closeness with Christ, a relational aspect, and a deep understanding of His love. That didn't resonate with my perception of Christ. How could I be close to someone so holy and separated from us by a heavenly realm? The verses spoke of Him working with power inside of us. I knew that the Holy Spirit lived in me, and sometimes I felt His power, but I didn't know how He was accomplishing things within me.

I was trying with all my power to be a better person and atone for my mistakes, but something in this passage hinted at His power and willingness to help. What was this fullness of life Paul was talking about? "Fullness" means filled to capacity, complete, satisfied. If God was promising the fullness of life, why did I still feel like I was wandering far away from Him, working to find Him in small moments, hoping He saw me from where He was. I craved the love that I was told He had for me. I desired to find the water to quench the dryness, but in all my years of following Christ, I still hadn't found the right way to meet that desire. I would have bursts of what modern Christians call their life-changing God moments, times when I received a prophetic word or witnessed a miracle and knew God was there, but I couldn't sustain those experiences. I didn't know how to understand Him or how He could understand me. What did it feel like to love God with my whole heart? What did that look like?

At that time, I was listening to a variety of messages from popular Christian teachers, messages on giving it all up for Christ, or finding your purpose and working for the Lord, but culture's focus on self began to warp my perspective of Christ. I began to look inward and ask what I was really doing for God. Had I laid all my worldly possessions down? What was I here for? If Jesus had died for me, why did it still hurt so bad inside some nights? If He loved me, why didn't I feel it? It became an endless search mission. I had so much to work on in order to be a better person. I was failing every day with my sin and hang ups. I had pain inside to deal with, and I didn't know where to start. God seemed so far away and quiet.

This was the beginning. It took this slight realization, a twinge inside, to spark a hunger in my heart to figure it out. And God was ready for me. I suppose He was waiting for it to dawn on me that He was offering me more—a promise of fullness of life. He said it in His Word. It was there for all of us. I recognized the difference in my life after accepting Him as my Saviour and believed that the change in lifestyle came from giving my life to God, and I was settled with that. But God was saying to my heart that He had even more for me. He knew I was hiding myself, buried beneath cultural deceptions and emotional wounds. He was a healer, and He wanted to emotionally heal me. He was a loving Father, and He wanted to speak to me as His child. He'd made a way for me to be with Him, and He wanted to get closer. As humans, we tend to linger in the dust. It's a dull existence in the desert of barren identity. I was there. Torn and wrecked by circumstance and poor decisions and loaded with pain, I was living in that isolation, afraid to uncover the real me. He was going to take me out of the desert so that I could discover what it meant to live in the fullness of life.

I was tired of the standoffs. After reading the verses in Ephesians that day, I felt like everything was finally going to change. It was time I faced God and told Him I wanted to know more. I wanted to understand the hard stuff in the Bible, the lists of names, the big vocabulary. Whatever it was I was missing, I asked Him to show me. He answered with that picture, the stump of a tree with a tender shoot. He told me He was taking me on a journey to uncover Him. All of Him.

We're told to love God with all our heart. We say we love God, and we sing that we love Him, but did I truly love Him? I wanted to fall in love with Christ. My heart desired to truly know Him. The love I felt for my husband and children was tangible—I could feel it and experience it emotionally. I sacrificed for my husband and children and thought of ways to love them more. Every day I told them that I loved them. But my love for Christ was different. If I said I loved Him, I should be doing the same for Him, feeling the same, sacrificing the same. Through God's love I was pulled from darkness, that much I knew. I wanted Him to know how grateful I was. What would have to change in order to truly fall in love with Christ? God knew my heart. In my invitation to Him to take hold and teach me, He was going to show me where to begin. He was offering me the gift of intimacy.

For many years I'd heard pastors preach about a quiet time with Christ, but I felt cynical about that. With kids and my full schedule, I felt that it was enough to fit in some Bible reading whenever I could. But now the Holy Spirit was keeping it at the forefront of my mind. I couldn't get away from the thought that I was supposed to make the time to do it. The standoff was over; the good guy was telling me to surrender. I decided to relent and set my alarm, waking up an hour earlier to sit in my grey chair and open His Word. Going through the motions of reading my Bible and praying felt odd. It was as if I was praying *to* God and not *sharing* my morning with Him.

As I thought about wanting to love Him more, I played around with the idea that I could simply ask Him for help. It might feel strange to ask for His help to fall in love with Him, but His Word told me I could ask for anything in His name. I made a daily habit of praying for my heart and mind to truly fall in love with Him: "Lord, I want to love you, actually love you. I don't want to just say the words. I want to feel it. Please show me how and produce the feelings of love for You."

Surprisingly, I felt no condemnation in asking; I only felt closer to Him. For a long time, I'd compared myself to other women and felt that

I couldn't ask for God's help in this, as if asking for help made me weaker than them. As I grasped my human shortcomings, it became impossible not to ask for His help. I had to put my pride aside and ask God what I was missing. As the weeks passed, I realized that my heart was growing warmer, and I began to feel affection for Christ—genuine endearment and warmth toward Him. In a short time, God had worked in my heart and produced a love for Him that I was unable to create on my own in my human flesh. In His grace, He gave me the ability: "*We love because he first loved us*" (1 John 4:19, ESV). As I felt a deep love for God growing inside my heart, I began to experience His deep fondness for me.

What does love for Christ look like? I think of David and the love letters he wrote to God in the book of Psalms. Each elegant psalm is poetry directly from his heart. He wrote psalms of self-discovery and psalms of thanksgiving. David was called the "*man after* [God's] *own heart*" (2 Samuel 13:14). Psalm 42 begins with a clue to this pursuit when David writes: "*As the deer longs for streams of water, so I long for you, O God*" (v. 1). It's a beautiful picture—a wild deer walking through the forest, looking for a spring to quench his thirst. This was how David longed for God. "Longing" is defined as a strong desire or a craving and provokes thoughts of passion and hunger. David searched for God's heart in everything he saw and did. The desire to know God and hear from Him drove David. His love for God went beyond a quiet time in the morning; his whole being was devoted to the continual pursuit of the heart of his Saviour.

A morning quiet time is our way of setting aside time at the beginning of the day to acknowledge the one we ultimately serve. It's a habit that serves as a sacrifice that tells God you will honour Him and give up some sleep to be with Him. In our fast-paced lifestyle, this type of quiet time with Christ is a necessary starting point. Intimacy doesn't grow from nothing.

But the Bible doesn't teach modern day quiet times; instead, it teaches a lifestyle of intimacy, the mindset of Christ in me. The people in the Bible didn't have a set time when they stopped everything and sat with their Bibles and a coffee and called it devotions. Their life was their devotion. God worked through people who laid their hearts down. They experienced intimacy with God as they let Him into their frailty and their weakness and literally gave whatever they could to God to use.

From the initial sacrifice of a routine devotional time grows an intimacy that settles between you and Christ. "Intimacy" is defined as a closeness, togetherness, mutual affection, friendship, and warmth. Making space to sit with Christ and open the scriptures is the first step, and the fruit of that sacrifice of time is rapport and wisdom. These two things change your life perspective and nurture your faith, creating stability in your spiritual walk. The fruit of this sacrifice is knowing God—really understanding His heart and allowing Him to see yours.

He already knows everything about your heart. He's just waiting for you to allow Him to speak into it.

This new space of intimacy with Christ is what I refer to as my Deep Place. It means to live in a space of defenceless vulnerability and cohesiveness with Christ. My morning devotions were the first step, and from them flowed rivers of intimacy and actual love for God and love poured out to God. I was finally discerning that staying in the Word meant that He was asking me to spend enough time reading and studying the scriptures that I would daily live them. It wasn't a chore but an eagerness to meet with Him and learn all I could about Him, because He was so important to me. It broke the lie that my misunderstanding of scripture separated me from God, and that reading it wouldn't make an impact in my life. I'd falsely believed that I knew all the stories already, and there wasn't much left to uncover. But God said that reading the scriptures was an invitation to a deeper relationship with Him.

My Deep Place is the space where He teaches me to live my every day. It's the area I occupy in my thought realm and heart. I unmask myself and pace with Christ in every moment, speaking to Him like a conversation in my heart, sharing comments and requests and fully believing He's there. No longer do I have my separate "God times," as we often refer to them. My life is lived in this Deep Place with Him at every moment. He is my *all the time* now. I seek to sense if He is moving, and I aim to hear Him speak. There is no separation of Him and me. His Word says that we have His Holy Spirit alive inside of us, living and breathing: "... *we know he lives in us because the Spirit he gave us lives in us* (1 John 3:24b). The notion of a separate quiet time with Christ seems odd when put into this perspective. The Word of God says that "*In him we live and move and have our being*" (Acts 17:28a, ESV). In Him we live. There is no separation. In Him we move. Again, no boundary between Him and us. In Him we have our being. This is how we are told to live. Blended with Him.

This Deep Place serves as a safe place for God to speak to us and lead us. We replace our personal agenda of coming to Him when we can with a commitment to live as one with Christ. He takes the landlord role over our soul. We don't want to make decisions on our own but turn to Him when things get messy. We want to know that God resides in every space of our being and will not fail us as we walk through each day. He shepherds us. It's the deepest sense of trust in Him, the full absorption of us by Him. It's a change of mindset. Christ isn't someone we go to; He resides in us and knows what we're thinking before we ask.

I've let Him into the space of my thoughts and heart and now have the deep sense that I am not alone, the profound truth that He is working on my behalf at all times, and the impactful knowledge that He loves me beyond my own comprehension: "*For just one day of intimacy with you is like a thousand days of joy rolled into one!*" (Psalm 84:10a, TPT). This God who passionately loves me, works on my behalf, and stays with me at all times is the God who resides in me and through me. It's a beautiful reality. It's my Deep Place.

One morning after I'd discovered my Deep Place, God told me to stay there. It was an odd thought at first. How could I reside in complete intimacy with Christ at all times? It required a change of mindset. I would wake up and remind myself to linger there in my Deep Place. God would whisper to me to stay step in step with Him and to blend with Him. These were key words in my transition from quiet time with Christ to all the time with Christ. I reminded myself to fuse with Him. We were one. Every moment I had breath, He was in me: *"Remain in me, and I will remain in you"* (John 15:4a). The Deep Place isn't a place to enter in and out of. "Remain" means to stay there. My faith became less of what I did and more of who I was.

Jesus prayed a beautiful prayer for us in John 17. He prayed to God from the depths of His heart, and through His words we can see His true character and feel the tender love He has for us:

> *My prayer is not for them alone. I pray also for those who will believe in me through their message, that all of them may be one, Father, just as you are in me and I am in You. May they also be in us so that the world may believe that You have sent me. I have given them the glory that you gave Me, that they may be one as we are one—I in them and You in Me—so that they may be brought to complete unity. Then the world will know that You sent me and have loved them even as You have loved Me.* (John 17:20–23, NIV)

These words are spoken out of the mouth of our Saviour. They tell of the plan for relationship and togetherness that Jesus knew was His Father's objective all along. It was woven inside His plan of redemption and brought to fruition with the arrival of the Holy Spirit after He rose again. His love for us, as Paul says in Ephesians, is wide and deep. He meant for us to be one with Him and God, and He prayed to God to make it so. This is absolute truth. We are in Him, and He is in us. We live as one with God and His son, Jesus. This is the space we occupy. Oneness. Our Deep Place.

In Matthew 25, Jesus paints a picture of the importance of developing our own intimacy with Him. He tells the story of ten bridesmaids. Five of the bridesmaids were wise and had extra oil for their lamps, and in turn were ready for the return of the bridegroom. The other five bridesmaids were foolish and didn't bring any oil with them for their lamps. With the return of the bridegroom approaching, the foolish five rushed and tried to borrow oil from the five wise women. The wise ones refused. They couldn't spare a drop, as they might miss the bridegroom. So the five foolish ones ran off to find someone from whom to purchase oil. The bridegroom arrived and took the five wise women into his banquet with him and closed the door. Later, the five foolish ones came and knocked at the door. The bridegroom told them that he didn't know who they were.

Within this story lies the importance of our relationship with Christ. It isn't enough to borrow from people around us who look stronger in faith than we do. We can read helpful books and listen to a hundred podcast sermons, but it ultimately comes down to our rapport with our Saviour. Does He know you? Do you have a Deep Place where you live in the gift He offers, a oneness with Him?

The author of Hebrews lists examples of faith, stories that give proof of a life of faith. Moses, Rahab, Abraham, Sarah, and Noah earned a good reputation through their intimate faith, because devoted faith leads to actions, goals, and decisions. Their stories aren't ones of major acts of accomplishment or esteem but of real people with a human nature. Christ recognized this nature and, despite it, resided in them. Inside this intimacy, people received their recognition. The gentle nudge of their Saviour beckoned them to move. That is the key. Faith intimacy motivates us, causes us to embrace ideas, and opens our hearts to receive a plan we wouldn't have thought up ourselves: "*Faith shows the reality of what we hope for; it is the evidence of things we cannot see. Through their faith, the people in days of old earned a good reputation*" (Hebrews 11:1–2).

The people in the popular Bible stories are commended for their intimacy, not their works. Yes, their works led to people being saved and huge movements in God's plans for mankind, but it began with their intimate faith. They were step in step with God and always listening: "*And it is impossible to please God without faith. Anyone who wants to come to him must believe that God exists and that he rewards those who sincerely seek him*" (Hebrews 11:6). A Deep Place. This is where we do our greatest works.

Intimacy with Christ begins with falling in love with Him. Take time to sit and be still. Pray for God to increase your love for Him. Tell Him all the things you're thankful for. Remember the times He came through for you, or you experienced those "God moments" and knew He was there. Think of Him as your closest friend and ask Him to open the eyes of your heart to see Him and know Him and to tear down the false humility that stands in your way. Meditate on these things and wait for Him to increase your passion for Him. Then stay there. Ask Him to stay step in step with you. Focus on Him and breathe Him in every day. Visualize Him inside of you and all around you at every moment of your day. Begin to accept the truth that He is in you, and you are in Him. There is no separation. This is the journey to your Deep Place. This is the first step to the fullness of life He offers to you.

REMEMBER THE GIFT: INTIMACY

Intimacy with Christ is a life dance, a place where you match His stride, step in step, cohesively. It's a deep space in your heart and the acknowledgement and true understanding that He resides inside of you. There is no separation of you and Him. He takes the lead, and hand in hand you go about the day, allowing Him to stir you. It's a sweet cadence of love.

PLANT THE SEED

1. When you think about your relationship with Christ, do you feel as though something is missing? In intimacy, we bridge the gap that separates us from Him. Talk to God. Tell Him how you feel and ask Him to fill in the gaps and increase your love for Him.

_____

_____

_____

_____

_____

2. Take a moment to meditate on the truth that you and Christ are one. He resides inside of you, and there is no longer separation between you

and Him. What does this mean for your life? What will this change in your daily life? Make a point of waking up each day and acknowledging that He is residing within you. Your Deep Place is a gift.

_____

_____

_____

_____

_____

Blossom Prayer

God, I long to know you more. I want to recognize your heart. Bring me into a deep place with you. Increase my love for you every day. Help me to make sitting down with You and reading your Word a priority. Please forgive me for not giving you my full attention. Uncover my heart, Lord, as I uncover yours. Thank you for giving your life so that we could be one. I accept your gift of intimacy and am ready to go all in. Stay step in step with me, Lord. Thank you for residing in and through me and leading me every day. Teach me how to live within my Deep Place at all times. Thank you for this gift. Amen.

Chapter Two

THE FULLNESS OF REST
—Replacing the Life Lived in Obligations and Depletion

It was a day like any other. I had woken up to an inbox full of emails, and a house full of hungry girls. Flipping pancakes, I held my phone as I responded to inquiries and fired off a few texts to my team. I announced to my girls that we would be heading to the donation collection room at the church to do some sorting, grabbing a new donation on the way. Rushing out the door, dishes in the sink and my anxiety levels rising, I buckled the girls in the van and backed out of the driveway. I called it "ministry."

Baby Blessings was an organization that blossomed out of a chance encounter. A response to an online ad for free baby items led my husband and I to meet a sixteen-year-old girl downtown. She pulled up in her friend's rickety old van and slowly stepped out of the passenger side, holding her swollen belly with her right hand. Never making eye contact with us, she accepted the items she'd asked for, loaded them up, and drove away. Have you ever had a moment when the compassion inside of you was so strong that the pull to do more took over? That experience left a hole in my heart that I wanted to fill. One look at that pregnant girl's lot in life and I took it upon my shoulders to be her saviour. I texted her and offered advice, rides, and more items. At first, she responded with short sentences, and then the contact faded. In exasperation, I threw my hands up in the air and prayed out loud: "Lord, why won't she let me help her anymore?"

He answered gently, "Help others." It only took a month before Baby Blessings was born.

The root of the ministry was born in purity. My heart had heard God. I did the most natural thing I could with the words I'd heard: I created an organization that gave essentials to more teens like this young mom. At first, it was life giving. It was exciting to rally my community to partner with the team in generosity and financial aid. I began to see myself as making a difference. It fed something inside of me that had felt "less than" or "not good enough." I was only beginning to find my Deep Place, so my misconceptions of who Christ was and what the cross meant weren't clear to me yet. I was still plagued with past regrets and shame stories, and Baby Blessings was a way for me to feel like I was atoning for those mistakes. I liked making a small difference for people.

With the birth of my third daughter, the ministry born from compassion became a dreaded list of chores. I began to feel buried in tasks to complete and people to respond to. My priorities were misguided, and I was replacing family commitments with ministry obligations. Overwhelmed and fearful of letting go, I sat in my Deep Place and pleaded with God to show me how to be free.

Modern church sermons, blog posts, and self-help books are saturated with the message of our "purpose." This can feed self-doubt, as we question if we're missing our purpose, or we worry that we might never find it. We want to hear the words, "Well done, good and faithful servant." Pastors and teachers who teach on finding purpose mean well. They come from a pure place and desire to genuinely help people avoid a stagnant life in Christ. But a thirty-minute sermon isn't sufficient for diving deeper into the love of Christ and how He walks with us. It's more of a quick pep talk than a thorough identity message. As a result, many of us leave feeling more confused than before.

Often the formulas for finding purpose have us measuring our time and talents. If we have time to volunteer, we should fill it. If we have a recognized talent, we must use it. Most of us don't have a specific talent that stands out. Not musically inclined or comfortable with kids, we start to think that God didn't create us with anything positive to contribute. Amid the noise of finding your purpose exists a nagging burden of comparison and unworthiness. Social media provides a lens into the day-to-day lives of people, displayed in the best way possible. Already confused and inundated with thoughts about the point of our existence, we have everyone else's purpose at our finger tips.

If you're part of a church or committee, you know that there's always a gaping hole of volunteer positions to fill. Most Sunday bulletins contain gentle "want ads" for good people to occupy. Each position is a noble cause, a worthy opportunity, and a need that warrants time and energy. We sign up for these spaces with pure and honest hearts, moved by compassion or the thought that it won't be too hard, and a scoop of guilt heaped on top. It isn't wrong to sign up for these positions or want to help your church or committee, but have you volunteered because God has highlighted this ministry in your heart? Has He made it obvious to you that He wants you there? Is there time in your schedule for this commitment? Is He partnering with you out of a place of rest to operate in that placement?

Let's get one thing straight: there is no formula for God's heart. We aren't meant to sit in a place of unworthiness and confusion. God didn't create anyone without gifts and passions to carry out the good plan He has for their life. He knows those gifts and passions and is waiting to uncover them with you. When you let Him in, when you surrender your person to Him and allow Him to speak into your heart and mind His vision of you, those passions will erupt from your heart and surprise you. We can't expect that such a mysterious God, who planned the stars and expertly designed the world, would create humans in so simple a way that they would discern their calling by the openings in their schedules. Our God is a master creator, and we are His ultimate masterpieces! He alone will uncover those brilliant passions and giftings within us. He wants to heal us, speak to us, and raise us up into all the wonderful favours He has given each of us to live a fulfilled life in Him. He is beckoning us to put away the "shoulds" and sit with Him awhile. He is waiting for you to listen to and accept what He speaks over you. Only then will good stuff flow.

The gift God wanted to offer me was rest. Rest is found in the stillness, when our minds and schedules are clear enough to make space to hear Him. It's an awareness of His presence and the acceptance that stillness is good. He gives us this rest in the promise that His sovereignty is taking care of everything. All we need to do is lean into Him. Our idea of purpose isn't God's idea. We consider what we accomplish here on Earth as our purpose, but God says it's about who we are. Our purpose is to live from our true selves and operate out of our placement in Him. It's the whole journey of our lives.

When partnering with God in the place of your true identity, you can't help but touch people in a profound way.

God says, "I created you to love me, and in turn you will love those I have placed around you." It's always about love. Viewing our purpose as a task keeps us wandering in the wilderness, warping our sense of worth.

God is gracious. He doesn't work on pressure and finish lines. Christians often look to Paul as an example of finding our earthly purpose. He teaches about a race and a finish line, but in Acts 20, he describes the sovereignty of God and the invitation to be our true selves. When Christ stopped Paul, then Saul, in his tracks and radically changed His life, he took him on a fullness journey. God changed Paul's thoughts about himself. Paul was the guy who'd made all the mistakes. He'd tried to murder the members of the new church and stop the spread of the gospel. He never would have thought of himself as someone who could partner with God.

In the wake of Paul's discovery of Christ, I'm sure He felt condemnation and regret. He probably wanted to work for Christ and atone for his mistakes. Despite Paul's faults, God still offered him a life of rest and a new identity in Him. That's what Christ does for us. When we physically make space and time to sit in our Deep Place with Christ, and fully engaged in an intimate relationship with Him, He begins to re-work our identity and align our thinking with His. God didn't say about Paul, "He finally gave his life over to me, so now I'm going to put him to work." What He did say was, "Paul, I see you. The real you. If you accept what I see in you and adopt my perspective of you, you will pour out my love to those around you and make a lasting impact." At first, Paul couldn't comprehend God's perspective of him, but as he allowed his Father God to speak life into the vulnerable areas, remove the shame, and expose the true Paul, he rose up into the pure, restful path God had prepared for him.

We'll never understand how God looks at us, or hear Him speak over our identity, if we don't make time and space for Him and for stillness. Paul allowed Christ inside his frailty. In the weakness, God poured His own capacity into Paul, and he was unable to go back to his old way of thinking about himself. He was purely transformed. It was always about reaching Paul's heart.

The race Paul talks about isn't meant to scare us into our purpose. It's simply how Paul describes His journey with Christ. God had placed tasks on Paul's heart *after* he exchanged his own idea of himself for Christ's. Paul was compelled toward his service because he knew it was tailor-made for him, and he was able to press on with the strength of the Holy Spirit. God knew the tasks that would fulfill Paul's heart, and through Paul's words in the Bible, we see that they did. He found inner contentment by sharing and teaching. These were the whispers of the Holy Spirit telling Paul to move. Your whispers will speak to your own heart's desires. We often mistake striving for perseverance, as the world teaches that hard work pays off. In the search for our one big thing, accomplishment, and recognition, the hard work turns into an unhealthy pursuit of acknowledgment from fellow humans. Paul understood that his audience was an audience of One.

We train for a race for months; it takes time, energy, and goals. God trained Paul ahead of time with the partnering of the Holy Spirit He'd placed inside of him. Paul studied God's Word, he practiced speaking to groups of people, and he familiarized himself with his Father God's heart by making space to spend time with God and receive from Him. Paul is one of the first examples in the Bible after Jesus ascends to Heaven of a life of intimacy with God. For Paul, the race comes after the hard work of training in Christ: "*All athletes are disciplined in their training. They do it to win a prize that will fade away, but we do it for an eternal prize*" (1 Corinthians 9:25).

Training encompassed learning about his true identity in Christ and how Christ saw him. It involved creating a relationship with God that was tight-knit and blended so deeply that Paul could sense in each day what Christ was beckoning him to do. The race was not a list of items to check off. He couldn't see the future, which was why he wrote that he would continue to press on until he finished his race. He let go of his human control, realizing that he could only do his best and let God be God. Only at the finish line of his life, in the deepness of his love and relationship with God, would he receive his prize of eternal life.

The only way to live in full freedom and know your gifts, talents, and worthiness is to sit with your Saviour and allow Him completely in—unprotected, defenceless, and comparison-free—you and your Father God, drowning out the noise from the surface and sitting in the deep quiet with your Father. This is the rest He offers in His Word, a rest that He died for you to have. In rising from the grave, He made space for us to live at a holy pace with a schedule that gives life and doesn't wear us down with to-dos. The lifestyle of rest that comes from giving yourself completely over to Christ is both serenity and accomplishments.

The author of Hebrews talks about this promised rest for God's people in chapter four. He explains that it's there for His people to enter. God prepared this rest for us, and all who enter into God's rest have rested from their works, just as God did after creating the world (v. 10). Picture it as a fork in the road. Moving to the left keeps you at your current pace, potentially overworked, tired, lacking peace, and craving down-time. The path on the right leads to the entrance to the rest God offers in Hebrews. It may look uneventful as you begin down the path. It may require the sacrifice of a few fun activities, or maybe the end of your service to a worthy cause, but as you tread along the path of rest, you can hear God in the stillness.

God's promise of rest brings with it a state of profound peace and an inner fulfillment like none other. It's a beautiful space where nobody holds obligations over your head that depend solely on striving to accomplish. When we pace with God in rest, our deepest desires are fulfilled, because we've made space for them to blossom. Our life begins to flourish with the dreams and expectations we hold inside that only our Father God knows about. It's a gift He extends to us as part of the promise of fullness of life.

There will always be opportunities to serve, and you can't miss your calling. God doesn't create us with our own characteristics and special qualities and then expect us to figure them out on our own. Breathe Christ in. Allow Him to tell you how He has made you. In that space, He will begin to re-work your perception of yourself and open your soul to new possibilities as He speaks words of identity into your heart. Chasing esteem and accomplishment, and the false promise of finding contentment in this, takes us off our own unique path. You will face a million fun activities to sign yourself and your family up for. You could live your entire life taking part in various lessons, church meetings, and committee events and not feel that you're missing out on anything. But you might feel the busyness and the hustle. In rest, we pour out His fruit; in rush, we sow impatience and discord. Rest is the only space in which to purely serve. This is about aligning your heart with what God wants to offer you and accepting the fact that nobody can do it all while doing it well.

It was the most piercing time of my life. My identity was so wrapped up in my "ministry," I didn't know if I could exist without it. I tried to imagine my life without the nagging to-do list and the drain of energy that was needed for my own home. My husband had begun to tell me that I needed to quit. My close heart-friends saw my empty tank and prayed with me for the strength to make the move. The hardest part was the confusion I sat with. If that ministry wasn't my purpose in life, then what was? It upset me that something so wonderful, that I felt God had blessed and grown organically from a place of compassion, didn't fit in with my normal life. If I wanted to keep looking like I had it all together, I needed to keep this specific piece of the puzzle connected.

Finally, something clicked inside my heart one evening. I had invited some close friends over to my house, and they offered to minister over me in prayer. One friend gave me some words of encouragement that took hold of my mind and transformed my thinking.

"God wants to tell you that you are not His worker, and He is not your boss," she said.

It all became clear to me in that one sentence of freedom Christ offered to my soul that evening. I was working, thinking it was my job to save the world. I was labouring, slogging, toiling in the constraints of the ministry I thought I was stuck in. God was trying to tell me that He wasn't as excited about my service as I thought He was. In love, He wanted me to know that He didn't like how I had structured our relationship. He didn't want to be my boss. He was my Father. He loved me, and He didn't want me to replace intimacy with service and call it my purpose.

That was the beginning of the end for me—the end of serving within that specific ministry, and the end of my purpose-driven thinking. I handed the keys and reins of Baby Blessings over to another partner. Even though Christ had moved me to take that final step, it wasn't easy. The world around me told me I needed my one big thing. Culture wanted me to boast about my accomplishments, and my human nature stumbled on comparison and service envy. As I processed this transition, I learned that the moment I left my "purpose," I was still me. I thought that if I left the ministry, I would be less of me than when I began. The world didn't crumble, the ministry continued, and I was still me.

The rest God offers contains many parts. With it comes the freedom to do nothing but sit at His feet and love Him. With His rest comes the invitation to make time for those we love and to honour connection over accomplishments. If you go days without speaking a word of meaning to the people you love, then you're not accepting Christ's life of rest. If your week passes by and you're unable to make time to connect with the friends or family members that bring you joy and life, you're not accepting the rest Christ offers. God our Father loves us and wants us to have time in our life for connection. The tasks we busy ourselves with should not steal time away from our spouse, children, siblings, family members, or friends in the name of ministry. Life in rest makes room to be with people and to have genuine conversations with those Christ has brought into our lives.

I now have a Deep Place where I host His presence and commune with my Father at all times. I can sit with Him as long as I need to and ask Him to tell me how He sees me. I can rest in the knowledge that no matter what I do, where I serve, or how I spend my time, He calls me to love Him first. He wants me to live inside rest and beckons me to enter in. What a loving Father to bring my life to a richer place than the empty hole of what I thought was my purpose.

God wants to give us permission to be ourselves—our normal, everyday, looks-like- everyone-else lives. The rest God offers says, "It's okay to be you." It's okay to be the standard woman and to live a typical day. You don't need to add anything flashy or glamorous to make your life anything more beautiful. This overwhelming peace transforms our thinking, and all we do comes from our love for Him. It becomes a daily friendship in which we pace with Christ and allow Him to prompt us when to move. God delights in our daily routines and offers us a place of confidence and contentment within it. It's up to us to agree with Him and accept that our life is not about the thrill or glitz but about our love for Him. From that perspective, every minute you live out the reason you were created. In Acts 17:25, we read that human hands can't serve His needs. God doesn't require you to do anything in order to feel useful.

Baby Blessings was a wonderful experience, and we helped hundreds of women by giving them baby items. I learned so much about working with a team and how to handle administrative tasks. We saw God perform miracles and provide the specific items we needed, and we gave the Word of God to each baby we blessed. Those were all significant moments for Christ, and I felt grateful to be a part of it. But when I was caught up in the routine of Baby Blessings and the volunteer work, I felt drained most days. When I left the ministry and what I thought was my purpose, I drew nearer to Christ. When I found my Deep Place with Him, I began to feel more fulfilled than I ever did doing that "big thing" for Christ.

Sometimes we believe that if the people around us could just look at us and notice that we're doing something significant, we'd feel affirmed. This fuels us to either accept tasks not meant for us, or to keep working in tasks that drag us down. When the crowd faded and it was just me and my Saviour, it became clear that His approval would confirm my worthiness, not the approval of strangers. My confidence didn't increase with every Facebook like, parade walk, or invitation to speak. I may have felt affirmed for a moment or two, but when the event was over and I was back to my ordinary life, the affirmation was gone and I was waiting for the next high of recognition. Christ recognizes me. He died for me. In the wholeness I feel when I am with Him, there is rest. Christ says I am worthy because I am His daughter. That's the only recognition I need. The writer of Ecclesiastes discusses the motivation of others to succeed out of envy: "*Better to have one handful with quietness than two handfuls with hard work chasing the wind*" (Ecclesiastes 4:6).

Be your ministry. Be you in Christ. That is your ministry. If you function from a place of intimacy with your Father God, allowing Him to tell you how He made you and to prompt you in your life moments, you'll experience a life of rest from where you will operate out of your true self. Blend with Him. Step in step. Cohesive. You were made for love: "*Yes, I am the vine; you are the branches. Those who remain in me, and I in them, will produce much fruit. From apart from me you can do nothing*" (John 15:5).

Psalm 23 contains the *flavour of rest*. Within its sweet and gentle words, David gives the readers the tender picture of what a life with Christ looks and feels like. I challenge you to read over these words and allow the picture and emotion of God's promised rest to penetrate your thoughts as you take it in. This is the flavour Christ offers for your day-to-day.

The Lord is my shepherd; I have all that I need. He lets me rest in green meadows; he leads me beside peaceful streams. He renews my strength. He guides me along right paths, bringing honor beside me. Your rod and your staff protect and comfort me. You prepare a feast for me in the presence of my enemies.

You honor me by anointing my head with oil. My cup overflows with blessings. Surely your goodness and unfailing love will pursue me all the days of my life, and I will live in the house of the Lord forever. (Psalm 23:1–6)

When Jesus walked on Earth, He had this flavour about Him. He didn't strive to frantically meet the spiritual needs of every person He met, and He certainly didn't fill His schedule so full each day that by the end of it He had lacked connection or joy. Jesus took each day as it came. If someone crossed His path and He felt led to heal or anoint them, He would. He wasn't on a "mission" each day to check boxes on His to-do list. He lived in a place of intimacy with His Father God, and inside that intimacy He carried out the tasks set before Him in peace and tenderness. His words carried love and goodness. He was so full of God's rest, His very presence caused people to stop in their tracks and sit at His feet to listen to His soothing voice of truth. He continually encouraged those around Him to go out and do what He was doing. He taught with grace and patience. Jesus walked a pace of rest with His Father God, knowing that the sovereignty of God was enough. He understood that God wasn't His task master with a list of set purposes Jesus had to get through each day. Jesus provided a model of the life we're to imitate now. God's Word says that Jesus came as a human to live among us and share our experiences. If we're imitating Him, then why were His days full of peace and meaningful connection, and our days full of hustle?

The key is to stop working for God and begin partnering with Him. This begins with giving Christ control over your life and making head space to hear from Him every day. This is more of a lifestyle than a daily duty. Living from your Deep Place, you'll be in constant communication with Christ. Rest is for the overwhelmed mind. Give Christ your schedule and ask Him to help you sort it out. Prayerfully consider every obligation you've committed yourself or your family to. Begin to weed out the ones that drown your family and take away from meaningful connection time. A life of rest says that connection comes before the extracurricular activities, because if we continue in our fast-paced lives, we'll miss out on relationship.

A life of rest allots time each week for get-togethers with friends or family. Ministry, service, and extracurricular activities don't keep you from these valuable relationship-building moments. A life of rest sees family and friends as priorities and makes space for them in your life schedule, eliminating their feeling that you're just "making time" for them. A life of rest says that God is your Father, not your boss. It accepts the slow pace of life and relinquishes the striving for bigger and better. It waits for God to open doors and tell you to step through them, not frantically look for ways to get in. A life of rest finds belonging and worth in Christ as His child. It's a full acceptance of "being enough" and living in Father God's love for you. All you need to accomplish for Him is to live a life of love— love poured out to Him and to others through connection to them both. A life of rest is a steady pace with Christ. It isn't a race. It isn't a panic. It is life in Christ.

"Belonging" is defined as a close and intimate relationship. We often think of belonging as an emotional pull, a feeling of fitting in, and the sense of confidence that comes with it. Belonging with Christ means intimacy with Him. All the confidence we need to live a life in rest comes from that place. With a clear and deep knowledge of our placement in Jesus, all Earth-led requirements fade away. When we know we belong to God and nothing can ever take us from His grip, we understand that there isn't anything He is task-mastering us to accomplish. It's inseparability. Like any good father, He wants to know you and spend time with you. He is willing to wait to reveal to you the assignments He has created for you, but He wants you first. Until you release yourself to Him entirely, He will keep waiting and patiently hoping that you will come to be with Him. It will always be relationship first with God. John 6:28–29 says it best: "*They replied, 'We want to perform God's works, too. What should we do?' Jesus told them, 'This is the only work God wants from you: Believe in the one he has sent.'*"

REMEMBER THE GIFT: REST

Rest is a pace that Christ invites us to enter into with Him. It's a gentle and tender lifestyle lacking in duties and requirements. The life of rest acknowledges the sovereignty of God and accepts that He desires a relationship with you first. A life of rest in God means making choices that align with what God is saying to your heart and mind, and offering up every area of your life to Him to sort out. A life of rest says that your purpose is found in your true identity in Him, and from that place you can't help but make an impact.

PLANT THE SEED

1. When you analyze your schedule, do you feel a general overload of commitments? In what areas do you strive? Take some time to offer up each area of your schedule to Christ and ask Him for wisdom. Invite God into your schedule and tell Him you want to align your heart with His plans for your life.

_____

_____

_____

_____

_____

_____

_____

2. Are you chasing the esteem and recognition of others? What lies have you been led to believe about the contentment that's found within your "one big thing?" Pray and ask the Holy Spirit to change your perception and pour truth into the areas that keep you chasing.

_____

_____

_____

_____

_____

_____

_____

Blossom Prayer

Lord, I want to enter into the rest you're offering me. I'm weary of wandering within this gift, so I ask that you please come and tend to me in this area I have tangled up for myself. I want to pace with you. Please forgive me if I've had the wrong idea of service for you, God. Lord, reveal your heart for me in this. Show me where I may be serving or giving of my time that isn't where you want me right now. Encourage me in the places that are. Strengthen me to say no to good opportunities that aren't meant for me and to keep my priorities in line with yours. Reverse my striving and give me your vision for my life. Help me to put our relationship first at all times. Help me to fully understand and accept that you love me no matter my accomplishments. Lead me to a full understanding of living with you inside rest. Thank you for this gift. Amen.

Chapter Three

THE FULLNESS OF IDENTITY
—Your Position in Christ

Right around the time I let go of Baby Blessings, I had a crisis of friendships. As I was discovering my Deep Place with Christ and began to change, I could feel the shift in my relationships with the people I spent the most time with. I could feel them pulling away, and it felt terrible and uncomfortable, which in turn left me feeling like I was sinking. Rejection is a painful process when you aren't standing in your identity placement. I couldn't go back to my former behaviour, as I could no longer separate my times with Christ from my times apart from Him. It made for some vulnerable hang-outs, and often I drove home from those get-togethers feeling misunderstood and confused. One particular evening I sat in my grey chair in the dark light of my living room and cried out to God: "Tell me who I am!" When the patterns in my life changed in such a drastic way, it revealed the ugly truth that most of my identity was wrapped up inside of my ministry and friendships. Once taken away, I felt undone. God in His tender mercy heard my cry that day and began to gently unpeel each layer of identity lies and to speak the truth of who I was in Him. I had no choice but to trust Him as I took each mask off one by one.

What we create on Earth for ourselves is far too fragile. God sees how we place things and people in our lives in a sort of pillow barricade, so that if there's ever a bump in the road, we're safely cushioned. I'd relied on the false comfort of my ministry and people groups. So much of my identity was wrapped up in what I was doing, and I based my self-worth on the approval of people. When we finally fall in love with Christ and find our pace of rest with Him, we acknowledge that those pillows must go, and we experience true freedom.

When my world began to unravel in the midst of my journey to fullness of life, I had nothing to fall back on. The cushions were gone. For years I'd identified myself as the person who ran Baby Blessings and prided myself on the stability of my friend group. God gracefully stopped me amid my own control and asked me to join His. The only stable standing I had was within Christ's spoken words over me. Those would never change. Although I had suffered loss, I now had the knowledge that He wasn't leaving me. In my loneliest nights, He told me that He was my friend. Though I felt the abandonment of broken human relationships, I had the best friend I could ask for—Jesus. He held me in His peace and love and told me that my life wasn't a puzzle of broken pieces to sort out, but a colour by number. He would tell me when to colour the next section, and when I looked back at my life, I'd see a beautiful picture. Maybe right now I couldn't see it, but He promised that one day I would. With that comfort, I pressed on and allowed Him to tell me who I was.

God made us with an innate desire to belong, evidenced by the way we try to find fulfillment through image, friendships, and talents. We want to matter to someone. Deep inside, we crave to be known and valued. For many years I battled an eating disorder. The more I got into weight loss and make up, the more people accepted me—even those who had rejected me in the past. This fed the deception that image and status matters. I never blamed those people; I blamed our enemy. He encourages a culture of "never enough" and insecurities. Everyone for themselves.

Since the desire to belong is woven so deep inside of us, it's no wonder we turn to addiction or self-destruction. We want someone to notice us. We want to feel secure. The God- given desire to belong is like a hole, but when we fill the hole with people and activities that come and go, we develop an unstable identity. God wants us to realize that He placed the need to belong inside of us for a purpose. We are His children, and He is our Father. We belong to Him: *"And I will be your Father, and you will be my sons and daughters, says the Lord Almighty"* (2 Corinthians 6:18).

As a Father who loves His children, God will speak the truth into who you are and why you're here. He will tell you in His gentle, loving way how much you mean to Him and that He chose you.

Your belonging is found in your intimacy with Him as your Father. That is your stable standing.

From this place of identity and true belonging we pour out, never denying our true self but rather flowing from it. Circumstances cannot break us down in this true identity; they can move and change, but we stand firm. If our intimacy with Christ is insufficient, we'll lack the love to truly touch people, because we'll feel love-starved ourselves.

God's Word tells us everything we need to know about who we are. God offered me the gift of identity, teaching me that there are two parts to understanding our true selves. The first requires us to accept His offer of full freedom in the wake of the cross. This freedom is the gift of righteousness. "Righteousness" means that we're blameless, no longer seen as the sinner we once were, but now without fault: *"For God was in Christ, reconciling the world to himself, no longer counting people's sins against them. And he gave us this wonderful message of reconciliation"* (2 Corinthians 5:19).

Reconciliation refers to a return to the relationship that existed between Adam and God before the first sin entered the world. Once that sin came, God couldn't stay close anymore, so He sent Jesus to reconcile, or reunite, us in that closeness. The Bible declares, not suggests, that through His death, God no longer counts our sin against us. He gifts us righteousness now. We often stagger at this point, unable to grasp that He has gifted us right standing in Him. Instead, we're stuck in a sinking view of ourselves.

For years, I fell into the trap of believing that I still needed to work on my moral standards for myself. I would forge ahead and study certain character traits I wanted to work on, or plunge myself into negative self-talk, such as "I will never change; this is just who I am." I thought I'd never be free from my human clutter. I had so much baggage and past history to work through, not to mention my lack of patience and selfishness. How could Paul preach that I was already free?

If Christ says that He has set us free in the wake of the cross, how do we fully accept and live in that freedom? In Philippians 3, Paul tells us that we rely on God, not human effort, and our faith makes us right with Him:

Yes, everything else is worthless when compared with the infinite value of knowing Christ Jesus my Lord. For his sake I have discarded everything else, counting it all as garbage, so that I could gain Christ and become one with him. I no longer count on my own righteousness through obeying the law; rather, I become righteous through faith in Christ. For God's way of making us right with himself depends on faith. (Philippians 3:8–9)

This is the open door to accepting that you already are right with God. Through our faith in Christ, He is changing us every day to be more like Him. There isn't anything we need to do to grow into His likeness except to keep an intimate relationship with Him.

Paul writes the most freeing and captivating verse on identity: "*Let me be clear, the Anointed One has set us free—not partially, but completely and wonderfully free! We must always cherish this truth and stubbornly refuse to go back into the bondage of our past*" (Galatians 5:1, TPT). Christ completed the required work for you to live in intimacy with Him. He took the shame, mistakes, and trauma and died with them on His shoulders. He came out of the grave on the third day, conquering each of your failures. He lives inside of you. Scripture teaches us to stop going backward and instead begin to understand that He is only asking you to be intimate with Him. In your intimacy, He will do the work to change the bits about you that seem to hang you up. To become more like Christ, all you have to do is stay in relationship with Him. The Holy Spirit will miraculously change your personhood and character. You are only meant to love Him.

Galatians is often referred to as the freedom book. Inside its beautiful chapters, Paul paints a picture of who we are in the freedom of Christ's death. At the beginning of Chapter 3, Paul calls us out for our mindless reasoning of never being good enough: "*How foolish can you be? After starting your new lives in the Spirit, why are you now trying to become perfect by your own human effort? Have you experienced so much for nothing? Surely it was not in vain, was it?*" (vv. 3–4). Paul stresses the fact that in our humanness, we believe that in our own might we can change, but in doing so, we say that what Jesus did through the cross was in vain. If we could perfect ourselves, He wouldn't have had to die in our place.

God wants us to realize that in His Son's death, He made the load light for us. It's not our responsibility to make ourselves good, but blame, shame, and the desire for perfection corrode this gift. God knows we'll continue to sin, so He speaks life into us and raises us into higher standing with Him. He removes the lies of shame so that we can flourish in who we really are. It's a package deal: "*… the Holy Spirit produces this kind of fruit in our lives: love, joy, peace, patience, kindness, goodness, faithfulness, gentleness, and self-control*" (Galatians 5:22). We can't produce these characteristics in our own strength. We could try, and they may last for a few days, but our human nature pulls us down again. When the Spirit does the work, though, the changes stick. This is a gift from God. This is freedom.

In Colossians 3:10, Paul says, "*Put on your new nature and be renewed as you learn to know your Creator and become like him.*" Our new nature is our new identity in Christ. No longer are we bound by rules and effort in order to achieve righteousness, but we are now seen as righteous because Christ lives in us. All·that Christ is, is now ours. When God looks at us, He sees Jesus living inside of us. There is still a need for repentance, yes, and the confession of mistakes and request for forgiveness. Real change, though, comes from fully relenting to the power of the Holy Spirit at work inside of us:

> *But you have received the Holy Spirit, and he lives within you, so you don't need anyone to teach you what is true. For the Spirit teaches you everything you need to know, and what he teaches is true—it is not a lie. So just as he has taught you, remain in fellowship with Christ.* (1 John 2:27)

When you're in an intimate relationship with Christ, you'll never hear Him say: "You did that again?" Instead, He says, "I know your struggle, and I am with you. We're in this together. Stay here with me, and we'll work it out. I am patient and kind, and we'll work on this as long as it takes. All I have is yours. You are not alone in this fight."

It reminds me of the story of the woman who committed adultery in John 8. Jesus tells the crowd that whoever is without sin should cast the first stone. When the accusers dissipate because of this question, He asks the woman if anyone is now condemning her. She tells Him no, and Jesus says that He doesn't condemn her either. He then tells the woman to go and sin no more. He refuses to remind her of what she has done and instead speaks life into her soul. He knows the power of the Holy Spirit that is coming to help her, and He partners with His Father in looking after her.

Once God revealed these truths to me in my identity journey, everything changed. I felt free as I unburdened the heavy load of my mistakes and faults. I could feel the difference physically and mentally. When my friendships and ministry changed and I had to look at myself in the mirror, completely stripped of what I thought made me, me, I saw someone with much work to do. But when God revealed that we were partnering in it, and all He wanted was my love for Him, the freedom poured in. I am already enough. Through Jesus, I am whole. With Jesus, I'm working on my kinks, but I am not the sum of my mistakes. The Holy

Spirit is alive and working on my mind and heart as I live in intimacy, and those changes can't be reversed.

Doubting our freedom is like asking a child what they want to be when they grow up, as if their whole adult life rests on what they will do and not in who they are. The child will be the same person when they reach maturity; they may decide to serve at a restaurant for their first job, attend college, and become a counsellor or work in trades, but they are still themselves. In the same way we desire to become more like Christ. As we mature in our faith, and the Spirit does the work inside of us, we become more like Him. In the meantime, though, we're still free. We might make a mistake one day and regret it, but it doesn't change who we are. We are still exempt in Him. We are still His child. It's not about what we do; it's about who we are.

It's a delicate thing to wrap our thoughts around the fact that God is the mighty and powerful ruler of the world yet also our tender Father. In chapter one, we explored the truth from Acts 17 that in Him we live and move and have our breath. That same verse ends with: "*We are his offspring*" (v. 28). You are His child. This was the second half of what He taught me about who I was in Him, and the same is true for you. He created the world so that He could create you and see you live here. It gives Him joy to see you alive and being you. Like any Father, He loves to watch you grow and change and simply be you. We aren't here to make something for ourselves and be noticed. We aren't here to live a glamorous life and constantly search for more:

> *Don't set the affections of your heart on this world or in loving the things of the world. The love of the Father and the love of the world are incompatible. For all that the world can offer us— the gratification of our flesh, the allurement of the things of the world, and the obsession with status and importance—none of these things come from the Father but from the world.* (1 John 2:15–17, TPT)

You are here because God wanted you here. He thought of you, created you, and loves to watch you living your life, surrounded by your people in the postal code where He placed you. As your Father, He gets joy from your simple moments, and He celebrates with you in your biggest accomplishments. Think of how we watch our own children at their school performances or riding their bike for the first time. Our heart wells up with pride and joy as we watch them doing normal, everyday-life things. That's how our Father God watches us. No matter the circumstance, He's your home to run to when you're searching for belonging. He provides and protects as a father. He shepherds us and teaches us what we need to understand in order to live in His promises.

In this knowledge, why would we think of God as an idol or some faraway god we serve and work for? He understands that without Him, we will want to fill our identity hole with status and material things, so He tells us in His Word to remind ourselves of who we are in Him at all times. Only He can fill the void of your identity. Tear down the barrier that separates you from Him. He is right there with you. In Him you live. You are His child. Your identity is that of His beloved child.

When I was living with my eating disorder, my nurse suggested that I check into an inpatient program at the local hospital. There, along with ten other girls, I learned about healthy eating habits, used art to express my feelings, took part in group therapy exercises, and learned about how to take care of my body. But there was no Christ in the program. I had no comprehension of God or His fatherhood at that time. I took part in every activity they suggested, but internally nothing changed. I left the program with new friends, a few extra pounds, and the same lies I'd come in with.

Freedom from identity lies only comes from the gift of identity in Jesus. True freedom for the mind and the victim of trauma can only be found in who we are as His child. I am in Jesus, and He is in me. His victory over death is mine. He died to free me from the bondage of my disease, and He died to free you too.

What flows from our identity as a child of God? All that Jesus is! Paul tells us in Colossians 3:12 that God dresses us for this new life of love in eight pieces of character: love, compassion, kindness, quiet strength, discipline, even temperedness, forgiveness, and humility. These illustrate who Father God is and how He views us as His children. Think about each characteristic. We're no longer bound by mistakes and past attempts at developing these traits. As His children, we claim these pieces of clothing as divine apparel that we never take off. When we slip up and are unkind, or have a moment of pride, we haven't taken these pieces off; we've only made a mistake. There is no condemnation from our Father. He shepherds us like any good father to do better next time. He gives us His Word to learn how others have made the same mistakes and how He helped them along the way. He may discipline us in order to grow us in one area, or change our mindset, but He raises us up. He never says we are hopeless or utters a negative word over us. He never shames us. He loves us with the same love He has for Jesus. We are Jesus's brothers and sisters, members of the divine family, and heirs to a kingdom.

Minutes ago, my oldest daughter, now eleven, told me about her lesson at church today. Cheekily referring to it as "doom and gloom," her take from the lesson was that she was going to mess up, but God wanted to be her friend anyway. She said the sermon was good, but it left her feeling like she'd never get it right. This opened up a good conversation between us, one that we've had before, but she is still learning. She feels like she shouldn't be a Christian, because she's going to keep sinning. This mindset feeds the feelings of condemnation and shame and the misconception that we don't matter to a distant God.

We must go back to what Jesus did for us when He hung on that cross. We'll never get it right, so Jesus made a way. Through His blood, we are fully justified and blameless in God's sight. All Christ asks us to do is love. Love Him first, and in turn love others. In our intimacy with Him, He changes us. It's stated right smack in the middle of Galatians 5 that the Spirit is guiding you now, and the Spirit gives you desires contrary to what the sinful nature craves. You are not what you do right, and you are not what you do wrong. Those are behaviors, separate from your identity. You are who He says you are: a child of God. He says you are perfect in His sight just the way you are, and He doesn't make mistakes.

While Christ was teaching me this truth, I received a prophetic picture from a woman on the ministry team at my church. She said that she saw me standing, and God was trying to place a new white robe on me, but I wasn't letting Him rest it on my shoulders. I was too busy trying to take off the robe I was already wearing. It had tears in it and pieces of fabric hanging down, torn and shredded. I was desperately struggling to take it off while God was gently telling me to keep it on and place the new robe over top. The woman told me that she had a sense that God was saying that the old robe was comfortable and part of who I was, and I was supposed to accept its place and put the new robe on top.

I knew immediately what she was referring to. It was a clear picture of what Christ had been gently teaching me. My old robe was my human life of sin, shame, and hardships—the junk I was trying to get rid of now that I was a follower of Christ. God was telling me to keep it on, because the new white robe fit comfortably over it. This was a pure picture of what Jesus did for us. We may still have sins we're working on and character traits we can't seem to pull off, but God says that's okay. He isn't asking us to take off our humanity and become some sort of angelic perfection. He created us as human, and He wants us that way. Jesus's death fits beautifully over our old garments of human hardship and slip ups. He dresses us in new clothing: kindness, strength, love, and the other traits we see in Colossians. Through His resurrection, our new garment is holy and blameless.

Many of us are familiar with Psalm 139, which states that God knows us and watches us. There's much to meditate on in this chapter about your identity, like how He created you and chose you before the world began and how He knows where you are at all times. The beauty behind each line of David's poetry here is that you are not just one among many. You are chosen, and this isn't something to be taken lightly. It's a big deal. "Chosen" means that you were selected, picked out, decided upon. You are enough to Christ, because He says you are. He is still completely satisfied with His choice, and nothing you do will change His mind.

Lord, you know everything there is to know about me. You perceive every movement of my heart and soul, and you understand my every thought before it even enters my mind. You are so intimately aware of me, Lord. You read my heart like an open book and you know all the words I'm about to speak before I even start a sentence! You know every step I will take before my journey even begins. You've gone into my future to prepare the way, and in kindness you follow behind me to spare me from the harm of my past. With your hand of love upon my life, you impart a blessing to me. This is just too wonderful, deep, and incomprehensible! Your understanding of me brings me wonder and strength. Where could I go from your Spirit? Where could I run and hide from your face? If I go up to heaven, you're there! If I go down to the realm of the dead, you're there too! If I fly with wings into the shining dawn, you're there! If I fly into the radiant sunset, you're there waiting! Wherever I go, your hand will guide me; your strength will empower me. It's impossible to disappear from you or to ask the darkness to hide me, for your presence is everywhere, bringing light into my night. There is no such thing as darkness with you. The night, to you, is as bright as the day; there's no difference between the two. You formed my innermost being, shaping my delicate inside and my intricate outside, and wove them all together in my mother's womb. I thank you, God, for making me so mysteriously complex! Everything you do is marvelously breathtaking. It simply amazes me to think about it! How thoroughly you know me, Lord! You even formed every bone in my body when you created me in the secret place, carefully, skillfully shaping me from nothing to something. You saw who you created me to be before I became me! Before I'd ever seen the light of day, the number of days you planned for me were already recorded in your book. Every single moment you are thinking of me! How precious and wonderful to consider that you cherish me constantly in your every thought! O God, your desires toward me are more than the grains of sand on every shore! When I awake each morning, you're still with me. (Psalm 139:1–18, TPT)

Can you accept your identity as a child of God? Will you wholeheartedly decide to leave the condemning route you've been walking and instead take up the gentle, loving care of your Heavenly Father, who calls you His beloved? It's time to shake off the "never enough" persona and just be yourself. His Spirit inside of you is working on your behalf. Paul speaks of this in Ephesians 3:20, when he writes that His power is alive and working within you. Stay with Him. Walk with Him in your Deep Place. He is changing you. All the glory is His. Accept the new robe He is placing atop your old one. He takes the lead and you dance with Him every step of the way.

Through my identity transformation, I realized that I didn't need to leave any friends behind or try to drag them on my journey. This wasn't about them. I was living from my Deep Place, walking in rest against any striving, and now I knew that I was free as His child. God brought women into my life who were able to shepherd me, as they had already accepted this fullness of life. Best of all, God became my best friend, and no earthly people or places were holding all the cards for me any longer. In Him, I would not be moved.

REMEMBER THE GIFT: IDENTITY

Your identity is as a child of God. Through Jesus's death, He made it possible to enter into His heavenly family. You're an heir to the kingdom, and Your Father sits on the throne. He dresses you in the character of Christ. When He looks at you, He sees all that Jesus is alive inside of you. Circumstances may change, but your placement in Christ never will.

PLANT THE SEED

1. Are you walking in condemnation that needs to be given to God? It might be a regret, a past mistake, a character trait you feel you can't improve on. Take time to invite the Holy Spirit into your soul and mind and, in intimacy, relent to His power to do the work for you.

---

2. Close your eyes and imagine God looking at you face-to-face. See His Father love inside His eyes as He focuses on you. Acknowledge that you are His child. Meditate on the truth that He sees all of Jesus in you. Partner with your Father God's perception of you and release yourself into the true identity He has gifted you.

_____

_____

_____

_____

Blossom Prayer

God, thank you that through your Son I am now part of your family. Please open my eyes to this gift of my identity in you. Reveal your thoughts about me, God. Increase my awareness of you as my Father. Help me to understand that all of who Jesus is resides in me, and that is the way you see me. Forgive me for walking in shame and regret. Help me to let go of wanting to do it on my own. Forgive me for the days that I wanted to give up. Raise me up into all that Jesus is. Holy Spirit, please come and do the work in me. Thank you for this gift. Amen.

Chapter Four

THE FULLNESS OF HEALING
—He Holds Your Heart

My schedule was emptier, and I had made my relationships my priority. I was now walking in a new freedom of who I was, and I was comfortably living in the slower paced lifestyle of just being me, knowing I was enough. Many mornings as I read God's Word, I'd think to myself, *I wonder what's next.* God had shown me so much treasure over the last few months that I was anticipating more good things. The fullness of life was slowly becoming clearer to me, and I finally felt like I was living with God instead of under Him. At moments I knew something bigger was coming. As my pace of life slowed down, I developed a clearer frame of mind. Sometimes the busyness of life causes us to ignore the challenges left from past hurts or severed relationships, but there's no real head space to confront those issues. There was more to me that I hadn't shown anyone yet. I had hidden places that hadn't faced the light. I knew I was God's child and that He loved me and I was here to love Him. In the promise of fullness of life, He was beginning to softly ask me to join Him in going deeper still.

I grew up in a home where I didn't feel seen, and my pain extended far down past the surface. I had lived through trauma and experienced the abuse of power from those who were supposed to be on my side. Within that environment, there was no room for authenticity or the ability to blossom into the identity God spoke over my life. As an adult, I was surrounded by people who had no idea of my history. I believed that since I was free in Christ, the past didn't matter anymore. This was true. My past mistakes were covered, and I was wholeheartedly free from my sin, but that didn't mean that those events didn't happen, or those people didn't hurt me. In the Gospel of John, God says that His light shines in the darkness, and the darkness can't understand it (v. 5). My buried hurt needed to be brought to the light. It was part of the journey to fullness of life, the gift of healing. He was going to help me reach into those places and bring the healing that was needed for me to break free and release the shame.

We all have moments in our lives when something internally breaks and the dark of the world begins to ease its way into how we view ourselves. Sometimes certain events change our perspectives forever. Perhaps a slight comment or the way we were treated left emotional scars. Whatever your case may be, there is a healer. Part of the promise of the fullness of life as described in Ephesians is to be made complete. "Complete" means whole, intact, and uncut. He knows your pain, and He saw who hurt you or what made the first cut. He stands before you now, a mighty healer, asking you to let Him into those wounds so that you can experience the transformation to fulfillment: *"Oh Lord my God, I cried to you for help, and you restored my health"* (Psalm 30:2). He answers our call for restoration and gently speaks life into the crevices of our pain.

When we accept full freedom in Christ because of what He did for us on the cross, we agree that He took our emotional pain and the transgressions that were committed against us. We acknowledge that He knew us and He knew that we were going to do wrong and be hurt by people. He wanted to make sure that we could find freedom and healing not only from our sin, but from the sins others would commit against us. We accept the truth that although in our humanness we feel masked, He sees behind the mask into the frailty of who we really are. Through the power of His love, we agree with Him that He can come and heal us.

He is the safest place where we can unload our hurt and ask the hard questions, like "Where were you?" The pace of rest we walk in with Him assures us that He is handling us with care, and He won't move us into any area of healing until He knows we're ready.

It takes bravery to let God in and expose yourself to Him. We tend to live inside emotional pain and think that we just have to get used to the discomfort. When we let God take control of our emotional healing, we tell Him that we trust Him. In our release, we let Him know that we believe in His goodness and deep care for us. He knows how to untangle the hurts and set us free. Exposing ourselves to God deepens our intimacy and strengthens our trust in Him. We are meant to give all our cares to our Dad.

One evening during my experience of healing, I was having coffee with a friend. I told her that I just wanted to be healed of everything immediately, like having a Band-Aid ripped off. I didn't like the feelings that came with facing my trauma and regrets. She calmly reminded me that God won't be rushed. He likes to take His time with me, and since He knows the whole picture already, I can rest in that. His Word says that there's a season for everything, including a time to heal (Ecclesiastes 3:3). In His perfect timing, He would take me through the process if I allowed Him to.

It was true. I'd been praying about confronting a family member who had hurt me, and I told God that I couldn't do it unless He helped me. If He told me when the timing was right, I'd follow through. One night as I was driving home, I heard Him whisper, "Tonight." I feared the unknowns. Whenever I was in the same room with that person, I felt the familiar childhood anxiety and defence mechanisms surface. I'd have to pray for days leading up to our scheduled times together. Since I lived from my Deep Place now, I knew He was in me and we were in it together, so I placed my trust in my Father God, and I went.

Driving over, I began to pray in tongues, as I didn't have any words to pray—I could only trust. I had to believe that there would be breakthrough that night. I sat across from my family member and was able to share all the things that I had stuffed down for years. At one point I looked across at him, and God gave me eyes to see him as a child. It softened my heart, and I was reminded that God knew him and wanted freedom for him too. That night was one of the most healing experiences of my life. I was able to forgive. God told me it was time, that I was ready, and we did it together. My loving Father in Heaven held my hand and told me that in Him I could face this. In Him, I was going to find the way out. I left the meet-up with a peace I hadn't felt before and a full amazement in my Father God.

Loving hard people isn't easy. It's much easier to cut them out of our lives, or decide that it isn't worth the heartache it would take to confront them. God takes us into healing with a new lens, one that sees the heart of those people and lends the perspective that everyone has been wounded and we're all in need of a Saviour. Because I forgave him, I could now live in greater freedom, because His power in me helped me accomplish infinitely more than I could have ever dreamed or asked for. It was another experience of the fullness of life from Ephesians.

Trauma ruins our ability to be vulnerable and let people in. When we don't experience healing from painful experiences, it becomes uncomfortable to speak about them. Shame swallows our hearts and minds, and we try to forget. But we have our Father God and His promise to restore us. We can rest on the truth that His death took our pain, and we are free now. We may ache inside and wish things had been different, but He takes the shame and guilt and says "It is finished; come into the light with me now": "*Let me be clear, the Anointed One has set us free—not partially, but completely and wonderfully free! We must always cherish this truth and stubbornly refuse to go back into the bondage of our past*" (Galatians 5:1, TPT).

"Bondage" is the perfect word to describe living in unhealed pain from the past. It can feel like you're completely wound up by a rope and you can't be your true self, because it's got its grasp around you. The enemy loves to feed lies into that grasp, saying that it's better to blame the people who hurt you and be angry. Even worse, he'll try to make you feel guilty over what others have done to you, which only tightens the hold and keeps you in secrecy. Christ came to set us wonderfully free, as Galatians teaches. We're to cherish that truth and stubbornly refuse to go back to the bondage of our past. He died for your sins, but He also died for your emotional and mental freedom from things beyond your control and from the mistakes you made or the ways you hurt people. There is a way to unwind that rope that has you so tightly bound in the secrecy of your story.

Shortly after forgiving my family member, I attended a women's event where my friend was the guest speaker. I bumped into a table of women I faintly knew from years past and chatted with them for a while. A few days later, my friend told me that the ladies had asked her a bunch of questions about me. One of them had asked, "What's happening in Sarah's life?" She commented that I was noticeably different—radiant, she called it.

When I thought back to when I had first met these ladies, I saw what she meant. Before I found my identity as a child of God and began my inner healing with Christ, I was tightly wound. I found it hard to make eye contact with women I thought had it all together, as I was so insecure and guarded. In my new-found freedom, I outwardly expressed myself differently. I wasn't afraid to be me anymore. I wasn't worried about everyone else's opinions of me. I knew who I was and that I travelled with my Saviour, and my healing opened me up in ways I didn't know were possible. It was an emotional and physical response. We don't realize what holds us down until it's gone. There may be parts of you waiting to be expressed if only you would accept the freedom Christ died for and ask Him to heal your cracks: "*I'll refresh tired bodies; I'll restore tired souls*" (Jeremiah 31:25, MSG).

I felt grateful that day. I could have still been living a reserved life, stuck in pain and shame. This new expression of myself, the freed one, was someone I had seen in others and desired for myself. God wants us all to live in that fullness. He is there and ready if you are. Paul says that "*… wherever the Spirit of the Lord is, there is freedom*" (2 Corinthians 3:17). He is in you. You are a resting place for freedom.

Jesus says, "*I have come as a light to shine in this dark world, so that all who put their trust in me will no longer remain in the dark*" (John 12:46). God knows if we're standing in the dark. He understands that because of that darkness, He needed to come and fight for you. His plan was to die to set you free. We're not supposed to be stuck living in shame and secrecy. There is power inside our stories and healing for our bodies when we bring them to the light. I experienced this reality when my husband and I were invited to dinner at a friend's house one Friday night. After dinner, we sat down with mugs of hot coffee, ready to get a little deeper into conversation. I was asked a question about my past, and I began to share. As I was sharing, my body began to physically shake. I finished my story, and the evening went on, but driving home I felt confused. I said to my husband, "I thought I was free of that stuff already." I was angry that the story still had enough power over me to cause a physical response.

Later that week, I relayed the event to a friend. She thoughtfully looked me in the eyes and said, "The shaking wasn't a result of any lingering negative power over you. That response was you stepping into new territory. A few months ago, you wouldn't have been able to share that story out loud with anyone. Now that you've found emotional healing inside that wound, you need to allow your body to get used to the light."

It may not feel easy right away. It might still feel awkward or scary to share your story, but feeling and freedom are two different things. Christ understands emotions. He created you with them. I came across a neat verse one day that reassured me of just how much our Father God knows our human body: "*Even if we feel guilty, God is greater than our feelings, and he knows everything*" (1 John 3:20). God understands the difference between what we feel and the truth. He is patient with us and never harsh. Your emotions may need time to catch up. He may want to work with you in one area of healing repeatedly until your heart and mind are completely free.

There are layers to emotional freedom that
take time, and God takes His time with us.

He is always resting His favour on us and wanting to help us get to the next level of freedom in Him. If you let Him into your weakness, He will lead you in rising up strong.

Lacking inner healing, we can begin to stuff ourselves down, hide from authenticity, and sow judgement and wounds in those around us. Without realizing it, we can negatively affect others. I found a quote on Pinterest one day that said, "If you don't heal what hurt you, you'll bleed on people who didn't cut you." Unhandled pain can lead to anger outbursts, withdrawal, insecurity, and fear. This affects the people we love, the ones who didn't hurt us. Before I dealt with my stuffed emotional pain, I poured distrust on people who had never given me reason not to trust them, and I leaked anger when I felt exposed. The complicated effects of inner wounds are so delicate, we need the wisdom of God to untangle them and set them straight. When we give God our pain, we're saying that in our deep love for our friends and family, we know it's not just for our benefit that we need to face the darkness. Rest assured, He wastes no pain. He scoops you up and transforms your wounds into beautiful wildflowers that bring the aroma of Him everywhere you go.

I have learned that the individuals who hurt me are just people themselves. There's always pain behind someone else's negative actions. I'm not here to judge those who live in the dark. I'm not able to be the Saviour and die to make a way for others to walk in the light, so it's not my place to decide who should pay for what evil in this world. I'm only responsible for myself, and I've learned that I only hurt my life if I stay in the shame and anger of my history.

"There is joy for those who deal justly with others and always do what is right" (Psalm 106:3). The right thing to do is to forgive. If it's too hard to forgive right now, then pray about it and ask God to make the way for you. God sees you and knows that your feelings will need time to catch up, but His grace is in the willing heart. Inner joy bubbles from within when you're set free, like the spring of living water God promises lives inside of us through Jesus: "Anyone who is thirsty may come to me! Anyone who believes in me may come and drink! For the Scriptures declare, 'Rivers of living water will flow from his heart'" (John 7:38). Letting go of the hold of your history is like the rope coming undone, sending you spinning around with your hands wide open in praise, joy, and thanksgiving to Jesus. It takes our eyes off the people who hurt us and puts them back on the one who saved us. He came for freedom—your freedom.

When I began to heal from my emotional wounds and to forgive, something odd began to surface in my soul. I wanted to pass the healing on to those who had hurt me. I wanted them to know the goodness of God. In John 13, Jesus washes His disciples' feet, humbling Himself in order to serve the very people He is going to die for. He looks them each in the eye and, in His washing, tells them they matter to Him. He forgives them, and they're worth the pain. I don't condone the actions of people who hurt others, but I am a sinner just like them. Jesus came and washed my feet like He washed theirs. It's a mysterious experience to desire good for those who have stung your soul. It's a new level of living like Jesus: *"So now I am giving you a new commandment: Love each other. Just as I have loved you, you should love each other. Your love for one another will prove to the world that you are my disciples"* (John 13:34–35).

Christ has given us a beautiful promise in the aftermath of our trauma. He will make all things work together for the good of those who love Him (Romans 8:28). Before I knew life in my Deep Place and my placement in God's family, I believed that this promise meant that no matter what I chose to do in life, He would make it work out. Now I know the beauty behind these words. God is saying to me, "My child, I know those who have hurt you. I weep with you because of what you have gone through and how it has changed how I intended for you to blossom. Those events occurred, and we're working through the pain together. I am on your side now and forever. All of what the enemy meant for evil, I am going to turn it for your good." He is our tender Father. The world may hurt us, but He will always win against the darkness. We just need to come to Him vulnerable, frail, and weak as we are, hands open and released to whatever He wants to do within us. My weakness is made strong in His power. I am blooming now within the liberation I have found in Him, despite my history. I carry with me an authority of freedom.

Shortly after God told me that we were going to work on emotional healing, I was awakened one night with a flashback of a childhood experience. Eyes open, I couldn't help but ask God, "Where were you?" Where was He when I was that child, unable to fend for myself and at the mercy of others. Where was He all those days that I was hiding, powerless and afraid? Soon I began to see pictures of people in my mind, like a slide show: past Sunday school leaders, school friends, and extended family members. He answered by saying, "I was in these people."

What a profound response. He was alive inside all of the people who made me feel safe and loved in small moments, just enough to see me through. Though I hadn't chosen Him yet, He had seen me and was taking care of me the best that He could in this broken world. I knew He hadn't wanted those people to hurt me, and in His kindness He'd brought others with His Spirit alive inside of them to come and touch me with His touch.

The experience taught my heart that I wanted to be a picture for people who needed the touch of God. I wanted to change my story into something brighter and make an impact on the people I meet. The kids at church and the neighbours on my street matter. We have no idea what another person's inner world looks like, but we know what our inner world looks like, and we have Jesus living in us. We have all the power of the Holy Spirit inside of us, ready to work with us to make a difference in the lives of others. Through love, which conquers all, we can be part of someone else's love story. Ecclesiastes 7:3 says that sadness has a refining influence. We may have experienced true sorrow, but it will enable us to empathize with other women and bring them hope. The enemy wants us to believe that we were forsaken, but God never turned His back on us. The only one who was forsaken was Jesus. God turned His face away from His own Son that day on the cross so that we could know the entrenching grasp He keeps us in. He holds us and never lets go.

Peter writes that "... *God paid a ransom to save you from the empty life you inherited from your ancestors*" (1 Peter 1:18). Our ancestors are the people who lived before Christ came. Now that Christ has overcome the cross and walked out of the grave restored, we aren't held back by any generations that came before us. We can break away and start a new legacy for ourselves and our family line. God promises to give honour to those who have endured suffering. In James, He speaks about Job, a man of great endurance. The Lord was kind to him because of his perseverance and loyalty.

"Endurance" means longevity and changelessness. I want to possess these qualities. There may be more hard times ahead for all of us, and we can't control our futures, but we can control where our eyes look to in times of distress. Looking to God grows our endurance, and we feel secure in the unchanging faith we hold to no matter what comes our way. The Bible teaches about keeping on doing what is right and entrusting our lives to the God who created us, because He will never fail us. In every circumstance, seek to stay with Christ. Step in step. Remember that He came to free you not only from your sin but from your emotional pain. He will never leave you. You're walking with Him wherever you go.

I was praying for a friend one morning, and God gave me a picture of her stepping barefoot across pebbles beneath the surface of a clear lake. The pebbles were painful under her tender feet, and God told me they represented the people and circumstances she felt she couldn't change. I saw God tenderly beckon her to come deeper into the water. There she floated peacefully, with the sun shining down on her. The pebbles were still underfoot, but she didn't feel them so painfully anymore. As we float deeper in our intimacy with Him, He deals with the pebbles underneath. We surrender it all, rest in His peace, and as our king, He takes the load of circumstances that seem impossible and gives us His easy yoke of love. Read these words from Romans and allow them to truly sink into your soul as you accept each line as a promise from your Father.

> And I am convinced that nothing can ever separate us from God's love. Neither death nor life, neither angels nor demons, neither our fears for today nor our worries about tomorrow—not even the powers of hell can separate us from God's love. No power in the sky above or in the earth below—indeed, nothing in all creation will ever be able to separate us from the love of God that is revealed in Christ Jesus our Lord. (Romans 8:38–39)

Through Christ, He tenderly cares for your wounds and leaves His fingerprints in the healing. He provides the peace in the circumstances that once brought anxiety and concern. Proverbs 14:30a says, "*A peaceful heart leads to a healthy body.*" Since God is peace, He is the perfect healer to bring peace to our minds and bodies as we lean into deeper intimacy with Him and let Him inside the pain.

My child, pay attention to what I say. Listen carefully to my words. Don't lose sight of them. Let them penetrate deep into your heart, for they bring life to those who find them, and healing to their whole body. (Proverbs 4:21–22)

REMEMBER THE GIFT: HEALING

Healing in Christ is restoration. Healing asks that you open your wounds for Him to come inside and rebuild into something beautiful. Healing acknowledges that He knows your pain and felt it on your behalf through the cross. Healing is His commitment to make all things new again inside your heart.

PLANT THE SEED

1. What areas in your life have you not allowed God into? Are there past hurts and remnants of trauma still in the dark? Think about the heart of your Father God for a moment. Invite your Father to enter into the dark spots now and tell Him that you're ready to come into the light. Ask Him for His help to trust that He is the perfect healer and is going to restore you in His perfect timing.

_____

_____

_____

_____

_____

2. Is there someone in your life you need to forgive? Think about that person for a moment and ask God to give you eyes to see them as He

does. Pray and ask God for a heart to forgive. Ask God to help you let go of any hurt or resentment you're holding on to that holds you back from revealing your true self.

_____

_____

_____

_____

_____

Blossom Prayer

Father God, I am wounded. People and events have hurt me, and I'm still struggling some days with the after-effects. God, I want to be free and accept your gift of healing. Show me how to be transparent with you and let you in. Help me to believe that you will handle me with care. Show me how to forgive those who have hurt me, and give me a tender heart to be love to those around me. God, tear down the lies and deception that I have grown to believe about myself, and tell me how you see me. Bring me down the path to complete restoration of my soul, no matter how long it takes. Heal me now in the wake of your cross. Thank you for this gift. Amen.

Chapter Five

THE FULLNESS OF SALVATION
—Understanding What Jesus Has Already Done

I was driving to a ladies' meeting at church one morning and having a conversation with God about some hard people in my life. I told Him that I wished salvation was easier to understand, because if these people just understood the significance of the cross, they'd want to accept Him as their Saviour. After a pause, I saw four words in my mind: making sense of salvation. Unsure of what the four words meant, I came home and googled them. A systematic theology book by Wayne Grudem came up with the title, *Making Sense of Salvation*. Since I'd seen the words so clearly, I decided to order the book.

As I read it, a whole new world of truth opened up to me. I'd been taught here and there about what salvation meant for me, but there were mysteries I'd left uncovered. I'd skipped over those places in the Bible, because I didn't have a full understanding yet of what God was talking about. I had no idea that once revealed they would have such an impact on my life and the way I viewed God and the work of the cross. I experienced a tidal wave of motivation to share what I'd learned. I decided to write a simpler version that would teach the truth I was so excited about.

In the book of Proverbs, Solomon, considered the wisest man of all, wrote scripture after scripture about attaining wisdom and knowledge. He boasted that without it, we were destined to fall off the path God had for us. Solomon preached that knowledge was good and wisdom was even better: "*Cry out for insight, and ask for understanding. Search for them as you would for silver; seek them like hidden treasures. Then you will understand what it means to fear the Lord, and you will gain knowledge of God*" (Proverbs 2:3–5).

When we find answers to our hard questions, walls crash down on our misconceptions about faith. You may have taken some elements of salvation for granted, or there may be missing pieces in your overall understanding of what salvation encompasses. In John 11:28, Jesus is referred to as the teacher. God gifts us teachers today too. We can go to these teachers and their work and glean from what they have uncovered. At some point we'll need to take initiative and find our answers. Take time to study and learn about the questions in your heart. God doesn't intend for His Word to feel like a mystery, a riddle too hard to understand. It's meant to be our daily instruction and guide book to fullness of life: "*Fear of the Lord is the foundation of wisdom. Knowledge of the Holy One results in good judgment*" (Proverbs 9:10). God tells us that in knowledge we have discernment to make good choices and stay on the path of righteousness.

Sometimes theology can make the Bible feel cold, or like His heart has been taken out of it. When scripture is explained in a simpler way, we see His heart weaving through the terminology as the mysteries of His power and love unfold. Some of the terms within systematic theology are written in song lyrics and found in Christian books. We sing the words without the full knowledge of what they mean. We read the words without slowing down to process the significance of what the cross accomplished.

Many times before Christ took me through my journey to fullness, I watched the people around me weeping while we sang about the cross. Easter came and went, and I could see in the eyes of fellow believers the impact it had on them. I didn't understand it yet. So far removed from Father God, and still walking separated from Jesus, I couldn't in my humanness comprehend how they connected so strongly with the story. Taking time to learn all we can about what the cross means helps to connect .dots. It's a story of His heart for us, a chronicle of devotion. Throughout the four Gospels, Jesus continually mentions that God is the one who sent Him to give us this gift. In today's Christian culture, there's a movement to forget about God and focus solely on Jesus. As we explore the fullness of salvation, it's impossible to forget about our Father God, as He performs these incredible, mind blowing transformations within our human bodies and changes the course of our lives. Here are the nine mysteries I uncovered when I went deeper into what salvation means for us:

1. COMMON GRACE

- Does God only allow good things to happen to His followers and bad things to those who don't follow Him?
- Are blessings only given to those who believe in Him?
- Does God answer the prayers of someone who isn't a Christian?

Common Grace refers to the blessings that come from God and are given to *all* people, Christian or non-Christian.

Common Grace doesn't depend on salvation.

Common Grace comes from *who God is*, not what Jesus did for the world by dying on the cross.

What should I know about the undeserved blessings that God gives to all people, both believers and unbelievers?

- life not death
- land that produces food
- beautiful nature to enjoy
- the goodness of people
- inward sense of right and wrong
- normal consequences of sin
- family
- government
- answered prayers
- the ability to hear of God

In the past he permitted all the nations to go their own ways, but he never left them without evidence of himself and his goodness. For instance, he sends you rain and good crops and gives you food and joyful hearts. (Acts 14:16-17)

2. ELECTION
- Why did God choose me?
- When did God choose me?

Election means He *chose you* to be saved. He created *you* and wanted *you*.

Election was an act of God *before* He created the world. He chose you before He began creating the first day.

Election happened not because of anything you did to prove yourself worthy.

Election brought God joy. He loves everything about you.

Election is proof that God knows who you are and has a plan for your life. You matter.

What should I know about election?
- Everything God has ever done was done because He loves you.
- Election is another reason to praise God, because He chose you!
- Election gives us energy to go out and tell others about Christ.
- Election is unconditional. God will never change His mind about you.
- We may not understand everything about election, but we have to understand that God is sovereign, which means He is the king and makes all the rules.
- We still have to choose God. He won't force us to follow Him.

"Even before he made the world, God loved us and chose us in Christ to be holy and without fault in his eyes" (Ephesians 1:4).

3. EFFECTIVE CALLING
- What does "gospel" mean?
- What is the gospel message?
- How does the gospel message work?

Effective Calling occurs when God speaks to us through the human message of the gospel story and asks us to become His follower. When we respond with a yes and ask God to live in our heart, we experience our effective calling moment.

What should I know about effective calling?

- We need to hear the gospel story first, understand the gospel story, and accept the gospel story to be saved.
- The Bible says that when we become a Christian, we come out of darkness and into the light. This means that sin doesn't have control over us any longer! We have the power of the Holy Spirit living inside us, and we are becoming righteous like Jesus.
- When we become a Christian, we come into a new place of peace, freedom, hope, holiness, and eternal life.
- The King of the Universe wanted to ask you to be in His family. You are desired and loved by God.
- There are four books in the Bible referred to as the "Gospels": Matthew, Mark, Luke, and John. They were written by four men who either lived and served with Jesus when He was here on Earth, or who worked closely with someone who did. They have recorded Christ's actions and words in those books. Each book includes the story of what Jesus did for us on the cross.

"But we impart a secret and hidden wisdom of God, which God decreed before the ages for our glory" (1 Corinthians 2:7, ESV).

4. REGENERATION

- What does it mean to be "born again"?
- What does "spiritual life" mean?
- What does "spiritual death" mean?

Regeneration occurs when God gives new spiritual life to us. This is sometimes called being born again.

Regeneration means that our old spiritual life, when we didn't believe in God, is dead.

Regeneration means that our new spiritual life is alive within us, because the Holy Spirit enters into our soul.

Regeneration is a secret act of God. We can't see it happen. This is a mystery.

Regeneration is something God does within us that enables us to believe in Him. Both God the Father and the Holy Spirit work together to allow regeneration to happen within us.

What should I know about regeneration?

- Regeneration is mysterious to humans. It happens in an instant.
- God has irresistible grace. This means that God calls (chooses) people and also gifts them regeneration. Both actions *guarantee* that we will say yes to the gospel story.
- Genuine regeneration will have a powerful effect on your life. It's like a spiritual seed planted in your heart that grows taller and stronger. You now have the power to stop sinning. It won't be easy, and sometimes you'll mess up, but now you aren't alone. You can ask God for help anytime you're struggling. You now contain the power of Christ to overcome the world and its temptations, and you have protection from Satan.
- The fruits of the Spirit are produced by the Holy Spirit working in you. They are love, joy, peace, patience, kindness, goodness, faithfulness, gentleness, and self-control. This will prove that God has given you new spiritual life.

And I will give you a new heart, and a new spirit I will put within you. And I will remove the heart of stone from your flesh and give you a heart of flesh. And I will put my Spirit within you, and cause you to walk in my statutes and be careful to obey my rules. (Ezekiel 36:26–27)

5. CONVERSION

- What does "repentance" mean?
- What is "saving faith"?
- Why do repentance and saving faith need to work together?

Conversion is our willing response to the gospel call. You decide to believe in Christ and resolve not to believe what you did before.

Conversion occurs when we sincerely repent of our sins and place our trust in Christ for salvation.

Conversion is nicknamed "turning." This makes sense, because we turn to God.

Some people call conversion by another name. You might have heard of saving faith. They both mean the same thing and include three things: we must hear about God, choose Him, and depend on Him. You can't have one without the other.

What should I know about conversion?

- Repentance is a deep, heartfelt apology to God for living in sin. You didn't know any better before He called you, but now you do. When we repent, we decide to turn away from our old sinful life and make a decision to do what's right

- Faith comes after repentance. It's the decision to trust God with your life.

- Repentance and faith go together.

- Repentance and faith continue throughout your whole life, and your heart seeks Christ. He wants you to keep desiring to do good and stay in relationship with Him. We continue to repent after we have messed up, because we know that's a heart after God.

- Faith should increase as our knowledge increases. As we learn more from our Bible and the Holy Spirit, our faith deepens, or grows.

"God saved you by his grace when you believed. And you can't take credit for this; it is a gift from God" (Ephesians 2:8).

6. JUSTIFICATION

- When are we considered free from our sin in God's eyes?
- How does our forgiveness happen?

Justification means that God considers our sins forgiven.

Justification is instantaneous! It happens immediately after faith, when we decide to repent and turn to God and believe in His gospel story.

Justification means that God now thinks of you as being righteous like Jesus. His righteousness, which means His pure goodness, now also belongs to you!

Justification means that when God looks at you, He looks with the same tender love as He looks at Jesus with. When God looks at you, He sees all the characteristics of Jesus in you.

What should I know about justification?

- We have no penalty to pay for our sin. Jesus took care of it. This includes our past and future sin. Sin isn't just our bad actions, but it's also emotions like anger and jealousy, or even complaining.
- Justification comes to us by God's grace, which is His deep love and consideration for us.
- Faith is the one attitude of the heart that is the opposite of depending on ourselves. This is why justification happens after faith. First, we have to decide to depend on God.

Yes, everything else is worthless when compared with the infinite value of knowing Christ Jesus my Lord. For his sake I have discarded everything else, counting it all garbage, so that I could gain Christ and become one with him. I no longer count on my own righteousness through obeying the law; rather, I become righteous through faith in Christ. For God's way of making us right with himself depends on faith. (Philippians 3:8–9)

7. ADOPTION

- Why do I call God my Father?
- Why is the church called God's family?
- What does becoming a member of God's family mean?
- Why do the writers in the Bible often call each other brothers and sisters?

Adoption is an act of God in which He makes us members of His family.

Adoption means that God sees us as His children. When He looks at us, He sees Jesus living inside us. And since the Holy Spirit guides us, we can become more and more like Jesus every day.

Adoption deepens our relationship with God. When we know that God calls us His children, we feel a deeper love for Him, like we would for a good earthly father.

Adoption means we can speak to God like He is our loving Father.

Adoption allows us to be a closer church family and have deeper connections with other members in the church.

What should I know about adoption?

- The church is God's family, so encourage one another and enjoy being together!
- We want to try to imitate God our Father. If we act like Him, we become more like Him.
- God disciplines us like a father. He wants us to grow stronger in our faith and become more like Jesus in our character, so we sometimes go through tough situations or life lessons. These are to help us develop.
- Being a child of God changes the way you relate, or connect, to God. When you pray, you're talking to someone who loves you as their dearly loved child. He wants to hear from you. He cares about your feelings, your health, your desires, your everything!
- Being a child of God means we have an inheritance from Him; something now belongs to us because we are His children. This inheritance is eternal life with Christ in Heaven!
- God our Father will take care of all your needs. Put your trust in Him for everything.
- God your Father loves to see you being you. He finds you beautiful in every way.

So you have not received a spirit that makes you fearful slaves. Instead, you received God's Spirit when he adopted you as his own children. Now we call him, "Abba, Father." For his Spirit joins with our spirit to affirm that we are God's children. (Romans 8:15–16)

8. SANCTIFICATION

- If the Bible says Jesus is in us, and all He has belongs to us, how do we become more like Jesus?
- What are the blessings that come from becoming more like Jesus?

Sanctification is something developed over time.

Sanctification requires us to partner with the power of the Holy Spirit to achieve it.

Sanctification makes us more like Christ.

We partner with the Holy Spirit in sanctification by reading the Bible, listening to the Holy Spirit, hearing God's voice, praying, sharing God's love with others, praising, building relationships with other believers, and releasing ourselves to Him completely.

What should I know about sanctification?

- Sanctification begins at regeneration, when God gives us new life!
- Sanctification increases throughout our lives. We are being changed into God's likeness through the power of the Holy Spirit inside of us. The changes occur in our thoughts, actions, and words.
- Sanctification is completed when we die. Our souls are set completely free from sin when we die, and we are made perfect when we go to Heaven to be with God forever.
- A Christian who never pursues Sanctification by partnering with the Holy Spirit and listening to His nudging will go years or maybe their whole lifetime with little progress in becoming like Jesus.

Now may the God of peace make you holy in every way, and may your whole spirit and soul and body be kept blameless until our Lord Jesus Christ comes again. God will make this happen, for he who calls you is faithful. (1 Thessalonians 5:23–24)

9. GLORIFICATION

- Why do we have to die?
- What happens if we die before Christ returns?
- What happens if we are alive when Christ returns?
- When do we go to Heaven?

- What will our new bodies be like?
- Why is Jesus taking so long to come back?

Glorification is the final step in redemption.

Glorification occurs when Christ returns and raises from the dead the believers who have died in years past. God reunites them with their souls and changes their bodies to be perfect resurrection bodies like Christ's.

Glorification is the end of our process of sanctification. Through it we reach full sanctification! Imagine that! No more temptation, no more sadness, and no more struggles!

What should I know about glorification?

- In our new bodies, we will see and act as God first intended us to when He created us.
- Our new bodies will be strong, have power through the Holy Spirit, always respond to the Holy Spirit, be full of light, and never age.
- Dying is an important part of God's plan to save us. In Hebrews 12:1, the writer says that Jesus is the pioneer and perfecter of our faith. This means He was the first to come and live out life as we do on Earth. We imitate all He did on Earth, because He lives in us, and that includes dying like He did. In order to gain our new, perfect bodies, our old, imperfect ones have to go!
- God never wanted us to have to die! When sin came into the world, we were no longer pure enough to enter Heaven. He had to come up with a way to make us pure again. God decided to send Jesus to give us a second chance at eternal life with Him!
- God wants to destroy death, so when Jesus comes to bring us to Heaven in our perfect bodies, He will destroy death once and for all!
- God doesn't waste the results of sin. He uses aging, weakness, sickness, and all the other stuff that comes with being human to teach us and discipline us. These experiences can help move us along in the process of sanctification.

And we believers also groan, even though we have the Holy Spirit within us as a foretaste of future glory, for we long for our bodies to be released from sin and suffering. We, too, wait with eager hope for the day when God will give us our full rights as his adopted children, including the new bodies he has promised us. We were given this hope when we were saved. (Romans 8:23–24a)

God wants us to know beyond the shadow of a doubt that He has full power, and His gift of salvation is more than a word—it's a beautiful series of discoveries. Understanding the process of salvation grows our intimacy and breaks down the walls of confusion and misinterpretation of our long-held views.

In view of all this, make every effort to respond to God's promises. Supplement your faith with a generous provision of moral excellence, and moral excellence with knowledge, and knowledge with self-control, and self-control with patient endurance, and patient endurance with godliness, and godliness with brotherly affection, and brotherly affection with love for everyone. The more you grow like this, the more productive and useful you will be in your knowledge of our Lord Jesus Christ. But those who fail to develop in this way are shortsighted or blind, forgetting that they have been cleansed from their old sins. (2 Peter 1:5–9)

God instructs us to grow in knowledge so that we'll be more productive and actionable. Salvation goes beyond our own selves. We are told to always be ready to explain our faith to anyone who asks (1 Peter 3:15). As we develop our knowledge of salvation, we will be ready to share the Good News with those who cross our paths. Isaiah 12:3 says that with joy we will draw water from the wells of salvation. The fullness of salvation is a gift, and it changes everything.

REMEMBER THE GIFT: SALVATION

Salvation is everything. It encompasses the whole of God's plan for us and chronicles His passionate heart. Through salvation, we are made pure again. It's our gift of wholeness, our gate to Heaven. Salvation says that we are members of God's family, and nothing will ever separate us from our Father again.

PLANT THE SEED

1. Make a list of the questions you have about your faith. Set a goal for a specific date and then work to uncover the answers to those questions. Ask God to steer you to the right places to find the truth you are looking for.

_____

_____

_____

_____

_____

_____

_____

2. Take time to ask God if there's an aspect of salvation that you have misunderstood. If He reveals a place to you, go back in the chapter and re-read the truth surrounding that aspect. Tell God you are ready to receive His truth for your life regarding salvation.

_____

_____

_____

_____

_____

_____

_____

Blossom Prayer

Heavenly Father, thank you for loving me so much that you sacrificed your Son. Help me to never take it for granted. Thank you for what you did within me when I first believed and the space I stand in now as your child. I pray that I will take initiative for my faith and learn the answers to my questions. Lead me in rooting my faith every day as I read your scriptures and listen for your voice. May my knowledge of salvation increase my wisdom as I live every day making choices that align with your plan. I am so grateful that I mean so much to you. Thank you for this gift. Amen.

Chapter Six

THE FULLNESS OF VULNERABILITY
—Wholeheartedly You

A desire for connection exists within all of us, whether we claim it or not. It's an innate, nagging longing for more. We feel it when we connect with another person, when something ignites inside of our hearts and we feel heard and understood. In our longing, we often mistake conversation for connection. An exchange of simple words, a get-together, or a meeting needs something deep to mold it into something more, but it often feels so uncomfortable, we decide to stay on the surface.

Why does vulnerability feel so gross? It makes me feel as though I'm standing on stage in front of a crowd of judges, as if what I'm going to say will cost so much, it's better to not say it. So I keep it in, convinced I feel better for it. Vulnerability can do something physical within us. It can cause goosebumps, a racing heart, fear, and anxiety. The stakes are high, yet deep down we know that vulnerability holds the key to true connection. It allows people in, and I want to be known. I want to be authentically seen for who I really am. It's a beautiful feeling to be known.

God gave each of us a story of who we are and where we live and what makes us uniquely ourselves. We love to hear the stories of others.

I've heard testimonies from all walks of life, stories of tragedy to triumph, or stories of regular people conquering new levels with God. Their stories can sweep us up and carry our emotions with each word to a greater understanding of how God loves us. Your story can do the same. This piece of my journey with God was the gift of vulnerability, to own my story, brave the audience, and let people in. He was healing me, and it was time to come out of hiding and share the ways that He'd brought light into my life.

I'm reminded of the story of Ezekiel and the valley of dry bones in Ezekiel 37. The Lord led Ezekiel around the bones and asked him, "... *can these bones become living people again?*" (v.3). Ezekiel looked around at the valley scattered with the dry and dusty bones. He saw them as they were, dead and discarded, and said to God, "... *you alone know the answer to that*" (v.3). Then God said to the bones that lay hopeless on the valley ground: "*I am going to put breath into you and make you live again!*" (v. 5). A loud rattling noise began, and the bones lifted up off the ground and became skeletons, empty formations of the life that once lived in them. Then muscle formed again over the bones. Then flesh. God told Ezekiel to speak a command over the skeletons and call for breath. He did this, and they all stood up on their feet.

This picture of the dry bones coming alive again reminds me of our vulnerable stories lying dry and dusty in the valley of self-protection. When I gave my identity over to Christ, He promised that no part of me was a wasted moment. He told me that I was a plan He'd orchestrated. Vulnerability to share our stories and experiences is a gift from Him. It's Him picking up a bone we wished we hadn't broken and saying to us, "Let me breathe life back into this one."

> *And I will give you a new heart, and I will put a new spirit in you. I will take out your stony, stubborn heart and give you a tender, responsive heart. And I will put my Spirit in you so that you will follow my decrees and be careful to obey my regulations.* (Ezekiel 36:26–27)

When I gave God my life, He gave me new life in Him. He took my stony, stubborn heart and replaced it with tenderness. In the tenderness flows the vulnerability. In the gentleness flows the truth.

It takes bravery to share your authentic self. I lived with a misconception of bravery up until that point. I thought bravery meant that you didn't feel scared to accomplish the hard thing you wanted to do. Bravery meant facing the hard thing, feeling fear, and doing it anyway. That makes someone truly brave. We lie to ourselves if we don't acknowledge that there are things we want to tackle in life but are held back by the fear of being seen, or the fear of failure. Through God's promise of the fullness of life, He has told you your placement in Him. He has called you His child, and He is healing your deepest wounds. You are strong in your weakness because of where you stand in Him. The most impactful stories we hear are from people fighting against all odds and claiming victory in the wake of hardships and trials. The interesting ideas, ministries, and causes are often born from that Deep Place inside of someone who recognizes how different life could have been without God. In vulnerability, there is power to be frail yet strong.

One of the areas I felt most vulnerable about was my appearance. I had set morning routines. My hairstyle had been the same for years, and my make up was exactly right. These routines stemmed from former habits. I had lived with my eating disorder from my teen years up until I gave Christ my life. The strict make up and hair routine was a remnant of that struggle, a piece of bondage that God wanted to strike down. I wasn't astonished that God wanted to touch that area, but it took me by surprise when He told me to change my hairstyle. If you're a woman who's had the same hairstyle for more than seven years, you can sympathize with me, and I'll gladly accept your empathy.

It felt intensely vulnerable to go through with it. My hair was bleached blonde all the way to the roots. My style took at least twenty minutes to get right each morning, and it held so much hairspray, it wasn't going anywhere in the prairie winds. God kept gently nudging me, though. He told me that He wanted me to know that I was going to be okay just being myself. God had taught me so much, and I was too far into my journey with Him to say no. Afterwards, I felt exposed. I worried that I wasn't going to be as beautiful or accepted if I was just plain me. I was trying to control, and God was saying to let go.

It took me a few months to really get into the new groove of a quicker morning routine and not going to get my roots done every five weeks, but once I was deep into the newness, I felt like I was soaring. It was another level of God's healing over me. He knew the hold that even a hair colour and style could have over someone; it went deeper than appearance. The hair colour had deceived me into a false sense of security. I'd let something material be a source my personal value instead of my Father God's spoken words over me and my placement in Him. He wanted to show me that in my natural state, He had made me beautiful. I now looked like my daughters, which was a delightful realization for my heart and one that God knew would be a gift to me. In the unmasking of the person I'd created myself to be, I found a new level of strength and freedom. Externals don't make us valuable—who lives inside of us does.

God cares deeply for us in our weaknesses, which is why He often uses the brittle to demonstrate His might. Vulnerability is about breaking restraints and relinquishing control. He wants to seep into the places where we feel our strength is greater than His. He asks us if we're willing to take a risk and trust that His way is best. In fullness, He asks us to let our guard down and let Him fully in. If there's an area you don't want to face, a dry bone you're ashamed of, let God know. He's your friend, your Father, and your healer, and He's saying to you, "Let me in. There's no need to hide anymore. I already see you. Let me walk with you into deeper freedom and bravery." He wants to uncover parts of your soul with you, and He promises joy within the process.

Vulnerability is about more than letting others see you; it's a key to hearing from God. When you hear God's voice, it comes from your soul, that Deep Place inside the intimacy you create with Him. Intimacy with Christ is vulnerability. It says to Him, "I am letting you all in, into the good and the bad. Take residence within it all." God knows where you need Him to unclench your fists, each area you hold on to with all your might. He craves speaking into the fear, distrust, and pride, those vulnerable places that, without Him, would keep you in cultural deception and striking. In the gift of vulnerability, Christ sees the openings and swoops in to fill them with the only truth that knocks down every lie of this culture.

His voice is heard the clearest inside the relenting of our plan for His.

One morning, my friend and I went to a breakfast being put on by a church in the city. She was one of the guest speakers and had asked me to come along to be her prayer warrior as she spoke. The tables were set for eight people, with coffee, tea, and pretty napkins at each place. We were sitting alone until two ladies we'd never met before came to join us. After some introductions and a bit of small talk, we learned that they were a mother and daughter who owned a local bakery and were in the middle of a possible sale of their family-run business. My friend looked me in the eye and announced, "Sarah here has a story to share with you about letting go of something. She's going to tell you all about it."

There it came. I felt that vulnerability attack—the goosebumps, fast-beating heart, and panic. My friend smiled at me warmly and gave me a knowing look. I said a quick prayer for the words to come out right and began to share my personal story about how God gently led me to hand Baby Blessings off to another team. I was able to empathize and share how wrapped up my identity was in what I was doing and not in my placement in Christ. It was my truth, and since I'd been set free, I was able to share that story.

The ladies looked at me and told me that what I had shared was exactly what they were going through. They weren't sure who they were without their bakery, and it was hard to let it go. We were able to pray together, and it was a rich experience of God's touch over us all. I don't know if they sold their business or not, but I do know that from a place of security in Christ, I was able to share, and the aftershock didn't strike me down. I was whole in Him. Psalm 118:17 says, "*I will not die; instead, I will live to tell what the Lord has done.*"

God had invested in me and broke the hold that searching for a worldly purpose had on my life. He took time to work with me and my heart, His Spirit empowered me to make a move and live the gentle life of rest, changing my life for the better. Why would I keep the story to myself if it could help others? To protect myself from stage-fright feelings? Confidence is built on little by little. Every time you push past the fear, there's a little more freedom to grab hold of.

I remember the first time I witnessed someone else's fruit of vulnerability. It was at the first ladies' Bible study I ever attended. I was sitting among ten or so other women of various ages. Our leader was a few years older than me, and we were studying a book on praying for our husbands. She opened with her brave story. It was filled with marital trials, child mishaps, fails, and wins. I was completely entranced in her every word. How God had taken what seemed impossible and made it all right again. I was humbled by her ability to be real with us and say out loud that marriage was hard and that she had experienced some tough relational issues with her husband. Every part of her story was brave. I imagined how vulnerable it must have felt, yet she spoke with such ease—joy, almost. Praise was woven within her brave story. His glory was braided inside the victories she shared.

I have added connection to my priority list over the last few years. When I connect with another human in a deep way, without secrets or false personas, I sense Heaven. Vulnerability has been the key to unlocking my true self, to experiencing the transformation of my story in Christ and seeing the evidence of how He makes all things new. It isn't enough to just know your story and keep it inside; people need to hear what you know, what is uniquely your truth as you've been taught by Christ. Share your transformations. You may regret what you have done, but you will never regret touching someone with His power through your triumph.

God promises to protect our vulnerability. Isaiah 50:4–7 reveals what God thinks about our brave stories:

The Sovereign Lord has given me his words of wisdom, so that I know how to comfort the weary. Morning by morning he wakens me and opens my understanding to his will. The Sovereign Lord has spoken to me, and I have listened. I have not rebelled or turned away. I offered my back to those who beat me and my cheeks to those who pulled out my beard. I did not hide my face from mockery and spitting. Because the Sovereign Lord helps me, I will not be disgraced. Therefore, I have set my face like a stone, determined to do his will. And I know that I will not be put to shame.

The Bible contains many stories of brave women who faced vulnerability and prevailed. Think of the story of Ruth. She decided to walk away from the chance to go back to her family and instead remained with her mother-in-law, Naomi, in Naomi's homeland. There was no certainty that things would work out, but she decided to do the hard thing and trust in God's promise not to be put to shame.

The Samaritan woman by the well who gave Jesus a drink also would have felt vulnerable, especially when Jesus pointed out her many past husbands and scorned life. She could have walked away and not told the rest of her town that she'd met the Messiah, but instead she bravely ran back, seeking to point others to Jesus.

Mary, the mother of Jesus, walked around unwed and pregnant, facing the sneers and questions of the people in her community. I'm sure she felt her heart racing and her knees wobbling sometimes, yet she pressed on and declared that she was pure. These women, among many others, were brave enough to share their stories and face the emotions that came along with them, all for the glory of God's ultimate kingdom story. Ultimately, it's all about His story. He allows us into His story, and we can offer up our own brave stories as an offering to Him: *"How beautiful on the mountains are the feet of the messenger who brings good news, the good news of peace and salvation, the news that the God of Israel reigns!"* (Isaiah 52:7). You are a messenger of good news, full of stories that lead to His love.

Jesus gives us a picture of how to live in vulnerable community with others. John 15 shines a light on how Jesus spoke and lived with His disciples. Jesus confides in them and calls them friends. He is real and honest with His friends. He doesn't hide behind a false persona, trying to keep it all together in the face of what He's about to do for them. Surely it would be easier on His disciples' emotions if Jesus just comforted them with lighthearted comments and encouragement notes, but instead He's raw. He tells them that it's going to be hard. He lets His friends see the real Him, the authentic Jesus always. In turn, His friends are able to express their worry and concern for not only Jesus, but for themselves after He's gone. They live in vulnerable community with one another.

Out of my Deep Place grew a new way to have community. Instead of attending a women's morning or a book study, I began to meet with a few close friends every other week. We take turns sharing what God is teaching us and where He has us in His Word. We share our struggles and our prayer requests. We let each other in on the hard stuff. Then we pray together: "*By yourself you're unprotected, with a friend you can face the worst*" (Ecclesiastes 4:12a, MSG). It's not a bad idea to have a women's morning with a larger group; in fact, we can learn a lot from a wide variety of people and age groups. This is different, though. These are my people, the ones who first saw my authentic self. As I let them in a little at a time, I learned that I can be my brave, vulnerable self with them. They are privy to the stories where I haven't yet found healing, and they travel with me on the journey. I pray that every one of you will have a few of these friends in your lives. In James 5:16a, we're told to "*Confess your sins to each other and pray for each other so that you may be healed.*"

Most of us can relate to being part of a study where everyone but the leader is silent. The leader asks a question, and we all shift uncomfortably. Some people look down, hoping not to be called upon, and others move their eyes from face to face, promising themselves that if someone else starts, they'll add to it. That is the fruit of the fear of authenticity. When we embrace our authenticity and stand in our identity placement, it doesn't matter if others speak up or not. We know we have something worth giving. We can learn a lot in a community of brave women who aren't held back by the fear of what others might think of them if they share their hard truths. In this type of community, we continue in the intimacy that Christ offers us. It extends from our hearts into the hearts of the people we share with. It brings closeness, connection, and the opportunity to feel truly known.

In preparation for a local women's retreat, I had the opportunity to write some pieces for the speaker to use as part of her identity talk. One piece that came of it was "Ten Daughter Declarations." These declarations align with our scriptural promises as daughters of God. We function from our authentic selves when we live in complete unison with our Saviour, knowing we have a Father who loves us. Read through these declarations and take time to fully believe each one. Memorize them. These are your promises as a valuable daughter of the king. We live with integrity and purpose as His daughters.

TEN DAUGHTER DECLARATIONS

1. In my true identity as a daughter of God, I express my authentic self (1 John 3:1).
2. My Father says that I am His special girl, and He has dressed me in royal robes of kindness, compassion, humility, forgiveness, discipline, love, quiet strength, and tender-heartedness (Colossians 3:12).
3. I am a valuable member of the kingdom family, and my inheritance is eternal life with my Father (Romans 8:17).
4. I carry with me the authority of my Father God (Luke 10:19).
5. My Father knows my needs and will always provide for me (Philippians 4:19).
6. The Holy Spirit lives in me, and through my intimacy with my Father, He is completing my transformation on my behalf (1 John 2:27).
7. My Father in Heaven approves of me. He makes my efforts successful (Psalm 90:17).
8. My self-worth does not rest in what I accomplish (John 6:29).
9. I have a story worth sharing (Psalm 118:17).
10. I turn to my Father first and trust Him with my circumstances (James 1:5).

Vulnerability says that I'm going to allow myself to be truly seen and trust that God holds my life and nobody can put me to shame. I will embrace exposure to Christ in order to tear down the walls of my confinement, and believe that what He has to give in its place makes way for liberation and joy. The uniqueness of who you are, the place you live, and your life experiences are gifts to share. God invites you to step into His spotlight, against the world's idea of fame, and gift your authentic self to someone else who needs you. This will not only strengthen the listener, but it will strengthen your soul as well. Letting go of our own control tells God that He has charge over us; it is an act of obedience. Don't miss the chance to surrender to Him. His strength is all you need to rise.

REMEMBER THE GIFT: VULNERABILITY

Vulnerability is the power to share your unique self. It's an opportunity to throw aside your human restraints and walk to a deeper place of freedom. It offers the promise that within your one-of-a-kind self there is freedom for other believers. Vulnerability encourages trust in God that He will protect you from harm. It's the unveiling of yourself in the confidence of who He is in you.

PLANT THE SEED

1. Is there an area of your life in which you're holding onto control? It could be your kids, financial stability, anger, or pride, among many others. What's holding you back from giving it entirely to God? Pray and ask God to come in and help you to let go.

_____

_____

_____

_____

_____

2. What is your biggest fear about sharing your story? Ask God to move inside that fear and replace it with His thoughts. Practise sharing

your story with people you feel close to. Ask God to open up new opportunities for you to share your story with those you encounter in your day-to-day life.

_____

_____

_____

_____

_____

Blossom Prayer

God, tear down the walls I've built up around myself in order to self-protect. I invite you into a deeper space with me to increase my confidence and the ability to accept myself for who I am and what I've gone through. Help me to praise you with my stories and realize that they are all for your glory, not my own. God, forgive me for the times I kept silent when I knew I should speak up, and give me new opportunities to try again. Release me as I share into deeper freedom. Reveal to me anything that's in my way and needs exposing in order to keep sharing what you are doing in my life. Keep my focus on you alone. Remind me every day that my authentic self rests in my identity as your daughter. Thank you for this gift. Amen.

Chapter Seven

THE FULLNESS OF POWER
—The Courage to Do What Your Heart Longs For

During my fullness journey, I was planning a retreat with some sisters in Christ to go away and relax, replenish, and re-focus. As I prayed over the schedule, I heard God tell me that He wanted me to share my testimony there. I'd never shared my testimony anywhere. I'd always wanted to, but I never had the courage. My life hadn't been easy, and I didn't want people to feel sorry for me. I was also afraid that people might think differently about me afterwards. I was still struggling with the feelings that arose when I thought about past hurts. I knew God had been working in me, though, and I'd been through much inner healing and identity restoration. I also knew my Deep Place, and that I wouldn't be alone when I shared. In the end, I agreed with God and said I would do it.

The minute I agreed in my spirit, the heaviness came like a physical weight. My mind went blank. My emotions turned to fear, and I felt stuck in place. I was being targeted by a cunning enemy who wanted me to stay in the jail of secrecy. I finally decided to call a good friend and tell her how I was feeling.

"I need your help," I said. "I'm so weighed down, I feel like I can't stand up and face my day. I know that my soul longs to share my whole story, but I'm afraid to let it out."

She gently spoke words of wisdom and light into the darkness, explaining that the enemy only had one thing over me—my secrets. His mission was to keep me silent and in hiding, and he was going to do everything he could to achieve that. "Think about the ripple effect of sharing how Christ lifted you to where you are now. Think about how that will help the women at the retreat who want to be open and share their stories. You're making way for the light."

It hadn't crossed my mind that the enemy would be involved. I was too preoccupied with my own protective measures. My hiding was his victory, not my defence. We prayed together, and the heaviness lifted. I was free again and more determined than ever. My God had saved me from that life. He'd rescued me and given me a new name, and I would do anything for Him. I began to pray for the courage I needed and the words to come. In His power, I wanted my story to be about His redemption and His victory. I wanted others to see Him in all His splendour: "*Then Jesus asked them, 'Would anyone light a lamp and then put it under a basket or under a bed? Of course not! A lamp is placed on a stand, where it's light will shine'*" (Mark 4:21). Jesus asks us to step into His plan and shine for His glory. What good is my redemption story if I hide it where no one can catch its spark?

In 1 Peter 2:5, we're called living stones, being built up as a spiritual house to be a holy priesthood and offer spiritual sacrifices acceptable to God through Jesus Christ. The central idea of sacrifice is surrender to God in the deepest place, our inner self. When we decide that no matter what happens, we're going to be courageous and do what God asks of us, we make a pure personal sacrifice. I was asked to make a spiritual sacrifice to the one who sacrificed the most, to come out of my denial, share how He broke my chains, and be a living testimony of how He loves us. This was about claiming new ground.

I prepared, and I shared. It wasn't magically easy. When it came time for me to lead the testimony session, I was trembling, but through the power of the Holy Spirit in me I was able to do it. Avoiding the hard stuff had kept me from knowing another level of fullness. God wasn't keeping it from me; I just wouldn't let Him in there. When I finally said the whole truth out loud, I experienced a new depth of Christ. There is a power when we speak the truth out loud. It serves as an agreement between what we believe to be true for ourselves internally and the physical world. I wasn't just dredging up the past; I was giving God the glory. I felt different spiritually and emotionally. I had finally let someone see the whole me. The whole story. My story. I had climbed a tall hill, looked out at the vast scenery, and stuck my victory flag at the top. It was a hard climb, but I'd made it with His help. I claimed another piece of freedom through the process.

Sharing at the retreat unveiled the realization that people aren't as scary as I thought. So often I'd deceived myself into believing that in order to succeed in social circles, I needed to be the one who had it all together. The strong, perfect one. My fellow retreaters still accepted me, and I actually felt like I could be more of myself around those women after that night, all because they knew my truth: "*Fearing people is a dangerous trap, but trusting the Lord means safety*" (Proverbs 29:25). Living as a sacrifice for God means denying our tendency to let fear win. He promises that He will see us through, and the goodness on the other side is so beautiful.

As God was teaching me about the fullness of life, He was reminding me that in Him I was brave. The word "brave" often came to my mind. I was walking in a new space, healed in some hard areas, fully resting in a good daily pace, and sure in my identity as His child. These breakthroughs meant that there wasn't much holding me down anymore. I felt like a bird that had been released from its cage. I was brave, and I could join with Him to carry out what my heart longed for. It reminds me of my four-year-old daughter. When the worship music plays in our home, she spins around and around, her arms stretched out wide. She looks so unafraid and unchained, no fear of the world yet. That was what God wanted for me, and He was revealing to me the gift of power.

I had dreams inside my heart—the kind of dreams you think about and truly anticipate as a child but then leave on the sidelines when adulthood rushes in with its failures, mistakes, and busyness. God was saying to my heart that in the fullness of my placement in Him, I was able to do more than I could imagine if I only agreed with Him that I was brave. Like sharing my testimony. I knew that woven within my story was a message of hope that could help someone cross some of their own barriers. Feeling fear, I shared the story. Feeling fear and doing it anyway made me brave.

Fullness of life carries with it a promise of a placement in Christ. We stand in new territory.

No longer are we slaves to the fear that once held us down, or the doubt that haunts us and mocks that we aren't good enough.

God says that in Him we can accomplish more than we think is possible: "*I pray that from his glorious, unlimited resources he will empower you with inner strength through his Spirit*" (Ephesians 3:16). We can stand on this. God is mighty and His Spirit is within us. He empowers us with inner strength to do the hard things, to accept assignments that seem too good to be true, to fight against self-doubt, and to rise above the fear. It's a life of courage. We can't always see His resources, as they flow from His heart into our hearts and minds. They accomplish what we can't always hear or feel, but when they're finished, we know that we have been touched by Him and are transformed.

Knowing where God wants to take you comes from your Deep Place. There, your spirit aligns with God's, and He can nudge you and speak to your heart. If you make time to hear from Him, you will. In rest, in your knowledge of your placement in His family, Christ has space to work with you. He understands what speaks to your heart, and only He knows His good plan for your life. He will move you if you relent to His power. There are good things awaiting you if you let go and let Him take you there.

Often, I freeze in the face of assignments, because I feel unqualified in comparison to other women I know. I will willfully opt out of something without an inch of effort. In 1 Peter 3, God teaches us to keep a humble attitude. My self-deprecating thoughts often come down to pride. In pride, I attempt to protect myself from discomfort, turning down opportunities so I don't have the chance to be embarrassed. What about the other side of the coin? What if the opportunities are a chance to practice standing in my placement in Christ and being courageous? How will I ever know what I can do in Christ if I stand on the sidelines? How do I embrace the fullness of life without stepping into the promise of inner power?

It reminds me of how I came into children's ministry at my church. I'd never considered myself as someone who would work in a kids' program. I knew that the program needed some leaders, and kids were waiting to join once leaders could be found. After Baby Blessings, I'd been careful not to volunteer right away but rather committed to praying for more leaders to step up. One evening as I prayed, I clearly felt the Holy Spirit whisper, "Sign up." I immediately went into self-doubt to protect myself. Was that the Holy Spirit or my imagination nudging me? I began to list the reasons why I wasn't right for the job. I was an organizer, a planner, and serving with kids meant busy evenings and crowd control. Not to mention the fact that I had my own kids to pour into. What I couldn't escape was that if the Holy Spirit was nudging, I wasn't going to be able to leave it alone or ignore the whisper. He was going to press on reminding me.

After a few days of trying to talk myself out of it, I signed up. The children's pastor met with me and said she wanted to put me into more of an overseer role, someone to help with organization and planning. After I'd spent a few weeks in the new role, the pastor, who by then had become a good friend, heard about some of the children's theology writing I'd been working on and asked if I would meet with her one afternoon to help plan some lessons for the kids. Later that year, I began leading the memory station, teaching scripture, and planning a mini-lesson for the kids each week.

I learned that I should have trusted that God knew me and had prepared a place for me specifically. He could empower me to do what He was nudging me to do. My heart's passion is for the scriptures and for everyone to have clear understanding of them. Through this ministry, He opened the door to fulfilling that piece of my heart. I asked God to forgive me for doubting Him and what He wanted to accomplish through me. I could have missed the gift. Philippians 2:13 says, "*For God is working in you, giving you the desire and the power to do what pleases him.*"

He never gives the whole plan. It's courageous to sign up and take the leap of faith. In my placement in His power, He will pour His unlimited resources over and through me. We are His messengers, anointed by His Spirit. He has people He wants to touch, and we have the privilege of aligning our hearts with His and being His hands and feet: "*But you will receive power when the Holy Spirit comes upon you. And you will be my witnesses, telling people about me everywhere—in Jerusalem, throughout Judea, in Samaria, and to the ends of the earth*" (Acts 1:8). We can rise up and be His ambassadors. We are not slaves to fear; we are strong in the power of His Spirit.

Our enemy wants to destroy our view of God and the placement we have in Him. He loves it when we're in the self-doubt cycle. He wants us to limit ourselves. In fullness, God gifts us authority to stand against the enemy and rise with all the power needed to defeat discomfort and fear: "*Look, I have given you authority over all the power of the enemy, and you can walk among snakes and scorpions and crush them. Nothing will injure you*" (Luke 10:19). This verse isn't referring to physical snakes and scorpions, but things like identity lies, shame, regret, limitations, and fears. In your placement in Christ, you have the authority, the inner power, to rise up and do more than you could imagine or dream.

The heroes in the Bible were human like you and me. They weren't gifted beyond our giftings. They felt fear and often tried to talk themselves out of where God wanted to take them. They couldn't see the whole road ahead yet either, but they took the first step. In our placement in Christ, we're heroes too. When you make that awkward phone call and invite a new neighbour over for coffee because God has nudged you to, you're a hero. When you obey God and speak up in a group conversation, even though you feel vulnerable, you're a hero. Every day we have a chance to be courageous in the little things, and every time we agree with our standing in Christ, we're elevated to a new level of freedom. In Him we are courageous. Stand tall in Him.

Often with good intentions we fall into the false humility category. We feel that the honourable thing to do is to stay meagre and needy. We confuse stepping into our strengths with pride, and then stop ourselves from doing what we fear may be perceived as showy. God says, "Yes, I see neediness and I recognize it and fill it, but don't confuse neediness with humility. You come to me with your needs and I answer, but courage requires bravery and a laying down of yourself to where I am leading you. It requires you to stand up and stand out." Through this gift of power, we have permission to stop apologizing for ourselves. We can take risks and make mistakes. God honours our efforts and works inside our mishaps. When we don't bother trying, He has nothing to work with: "*Hope deferred makes the heart sick, but a dream fulfilled is a tree of life*" (Proverbs 13:12). He invites us to bloom in His power.

The book of Acts is full of stories of people who were courageous through the Holy Spirit. Jesus had just ascended to Heaven and had promised to send a helper, His Spirit, to new believers to empower them to carry on what He had started on Earth. Acts begins with Peter preaching in the temple. Peter saw His opportunity and addressed the crowd (Acts 3). In turn, members of the council were impressed by the boldness of Peter and John. They recognized that they were ordinary men with no special training, yet they left such an impact. This wasn't the result of human strength but of the power of the Holy Spirit in them. Other believers, inspired by John and Peter, prayed for the Holy Spirit to help them as well and began to preach the Word of God with boldness.

This was a courage story. First Peter, then John, and now the new believers were emboldened to share. This happens when we unite with the Holy Spirit. He gives us boldness, which is passed on to those around us as we inspire them with our stories. Jesus planned for us to spread His message by telling others about it. In Acts 13, we read about one of the first church services after Jesus left. Those in charge read from the book of Moses and then said, "*Brothers, if you have any word of encouragement for the people, come and give it*" (v. 15). Many stories exist about the first believers strengthening and encouraging each other with words. Our lives are meant to be an offering poured out; our days not laid to waste. Share your words and join with Jesus's plan to strengthen fellow believers. Every leap of courage speaks of His power within you. Just like Peter and John, we can pray and ask for the boldness we need.

During my inner healing process, God told me that we were going to face my fear of leaving my kids. I had left them here and there for a weekend, either with my husband or in-laws, but I'd never left them for a longer time-frame and gone away with my husband. A work trip came up, and my husband excitedly asked me to join him for the week in Banff, Alberta. The opportunity sounded so good; it's a beautiful area, and our hotel was a castle-like building situated in the mountains. I wanted to say yes, but it was too hard. When you experience fear as a direct result of trauma, it feels reasonable to you.

I was eleven when I was left alone in a casino lounge so that a family member could go inside to play the slots. He promised that he'd be back in an hour, and then asked the bartender to keep an eye on me. I remember sitting there as the hours passed by, and the intensity of the emotion I felt as the physical discomfort grew. I couldn't put into words at eleven what the anxiety and fear mixed together felt like, but as an adult I know I was experiencing the emotions of abandonment. I was acutely aware of being surrounded by strangers and wishing that my family member would come back. When he finally did, it was hours later, and I obediently walked out beside him without questioning what had happened.

This childhood event left a permanent mark on my brain and inner emotional world. I needed God to heal me, because the inner workings were so delicate, I didn't know where to begin. I never wanted to leave my children, because I'd been left as a child, and I was going to do better by them. It was a mental stronghold. If I left them, and something happened to me or them, I would never forgive myself. If I stayed with them, everything would be in my control. I protected my family fiercely, as I was amazed at the wonderful life I now had. Even though I knew that God had given me this life, I wasn't ready to trust Him with my kids quite yet.

I prayed for weeks about it, and God kept whispering for me to go. He told me to trust Him and that there was beauty for my marriage and children on the other side. It was time. We're always healed in His perfect timing. I booked the trip and began the weeks of anxiety. I talked about it wherever I went, trying to find someone to convince me that my reasons for staying home were valid. As I type this, I know I was being ridiculous, but those strongholds feel so real until they're broken. You might be thinking of one right now. It could be wearing make up wherever you go, afraid of people seeing your raw self. It might be financial control, or keeping up appearances. Whatever it may be, God gifts us the power to break free as part of His fullness.

The worst part of my experience was walking down the corridor that led into the plane. I asked my husband if I could please turn back. He took my hand and we kept going. Driving in the shuttle to the resort, I had my ear buds in and my Bethel music blaring as I stared out the window. I could feel my strength growing with every mile—the tall mountains soaring around me, the magnitude of God's sovereignty overwhelming. I felt the fear, but I was doing it anyway. I was brave.

Every day in Banff I journalled what God was revealing to me in my separation from my routine. He told me that He loved the girls more than I did, and that He loved me just the same. In His power, I conquered. You have the power within you too. Tell Him that you're ready for Him to take control and release the power to fulfill your heart and break strongholds now. Trust God's timing. He knows where you're at and presents the opportunities when He trusts your heart is ready. Every time you conquer a little bit of the fear with His power, you bloom.

Last winter another work trip came up, this time to Africa. I immediately thought that it was a trip of a lifetime and felt pretty sure that God was giving it to us as a gift. Though I had conquered Banff for the week, I wasn't sure I could leave the continent, and the comfortable fear began to inch its way in a little. When I went to God in prayer, He surprised me. He told me the trip wasn't for me. He knew my heart, and it wasn't time. I may have His power, but He has the timing. One day I will go to Africa. Right now, God says He's still working it out in me. I don't have to be completely strong enough after one victory. Fullness is a journey with Him; it keeps going. He turns pain into power. I love that He knows me so well and is taking care of me. He is a good Father.

In Philippians 1:6, Paul says, *"And I am certain that God, who began the good work within you, will continue his work until it is finally finished on the day when Christ Jesus returns."* Agree in your heart that He knows what you long for and He wants to walk with you until completion. He began the work in you when He dreamed of you. He lovingly thought up each part of you, including your passions and what makes you feel alive. He promises that He will see you into the fullness of your placement in Him, if you let Him. Let His nudging take you deeper into fullness with Him. He delights in our victories.

As you're reading this, you might be thinking: "She has a book published, so of course she can speak of doing the hard stuff and being brave. It's all worked out for her." Here's the thing: this manuscript isn't published as I write this, and as I type these words, I'm not sure it ever will be. Every day I come to my computer and push past the doubts and the "I'm not good enough" self-talk and press on, reminding myself that I felt the Spirit's nudging. If I don't take this risk, I close every possibility. If I at least try, I'll never regret giving it my best shot. I am no longer living to accomplish something great. I am living in rest as His child. Whether published or not, I'm still me.

Before I found fullness, I doubted everything. But even if this book is never bound or seen on a shelf somewhere, all that matters is Him. He loves watching me write this, research, and study. He enjoys witnessing me trying to relay what I learn. It's been fun to sit with Him here, at the same desk every afternoon. The process is the gift. I am fulfilling a passion inside my own soul as I write each page, and He knows my heart. If you're reading this as a real book, remember that I am just a normal girl, part of the same kingdom family as you, trying with the inner power He places inside me to create something beautiful for Him. We are brave sisters, and our Father God can accomplish in us more than we could ever dream for ourselves.

REMEMBER THE GIFT: POWER
Power is the Holy Spirit residing inside of you, bringing you to new places and increasing your territory. The gift of power says that what your heart

longs for, He will give you the courage to do in His timing. Power invites you into opportunities that you wouldn't have let yourself into without Him. It allows a trust between you and God. He knows your future, and He is taking you on a beautiful journey that fulfills your heart.

PLANT THE SEED

1. Are there things in your heart that you're longing to do or experience? What are those things? Do you believe that God wants to partner with you to fulfill your heart's desires? Ask God to come in and fill you with His Spirit and the gift of power. Tell God that you desire to hear the nudging louder, and you're excited to take courageous steps with Him.

_____

_____

_____

_____

_____

_____

_____

2. Are you struggling with false humility and trying to save face? What are the lies that keep you in that mindset? Invite your Father God to speak against the lies and replace them with His thoughts about you. Allow yourself the permission in your new standing in Him to take risks and make mistakes. Give Him something to work with.

_____

_____

_____

_____

_____

_____

_____

Blossom Prayer

Father God, thank you that you know my heart. Thank you that you always want to fill me with all of your goodness. Lord, open my understanding of the power of the Holy Spirit inside of me. Increase my awareness of You to notice when you're asking me to move. Forgive me for doubting myself. Help me to accept that in you I can do more than I ever imagined. Thank you for the places you are taking me into that are meant to fill my heart in the unique way you created me for. Lord, thank you for this gift. Amen.

Chapter Eight

THE FULLNESS OF TIME
—He Is Devoted to You

We recently moved out of a house we'd lived in for ten years. Our old house was a gift, the fulfillment of a dream. I remember walking through it the day we were going to make the offer. I was eight months pregnant with our second daughter and thinking to myself, *Our girls are going to be so lucky to grow up in this home.* It was a feeling, a knowing, that the house was a blessing not to be taken lightly. I was grateful for it.

While living in that home, I decided to take a prophetic ministry course at our church. During one class, a man came up to me with a drawing of a house, and he told me that God had given him that picture for me. I scrutinized the sketch and tried to figure out whose house it was. Maybe it was our current home, but just a little off. Unsure of what it stood for, I tucked it in my closet at home and forgot about it.

Five years and a third daughter later, we were feeling cramped and disorganized and needed more space as our girls grew into the pre-teen years. Addicted to memories, my husband and I spent many evenings on our deck, contemplating the right thing to do. We knew the gift our home had been to us. We understood that we could make it work, and also the effect leaving the neighbourhood would have on our kids, who had made friends there. After touring multiple homes with no success, a house that had come down in price on the market came to our attention. When we walked inside for the first time, it immediately felt like ours. My husband and I looked at each other with a knowing look. We were going to make an offer and try to make it ours for real.

After we bought the house, God reminded me of the picture I'd been given so many years before. A wash of love came over me as the realization hit: the picture was of the house we'd just purchased. It had the same roof line, trees in the yard, and windows. I was overwhelmed with God's devotion to me. He really knew me. He'd taken time years earlier so that at that moment, I'd be reminded again that He knows my steps and sees me. This is the area of fullness of time He gifts to us. He is fully aware of you and completely in awe of you. He is present for you in every second of your day. He is right here, and you have His full attention.

John writes of this deep love and attentiveness: "*We know how much God loves us, and we have put our trust in his love. God is love, and all who live in love live in God, and God lives in them*" (1 John 4:16). God's whole being is love, and He always operates from a love perspective. "Love" is defined as tenderness and warmth, like the intimacy He gifts us in fullness. Your Father God continually functions from that space of warmth and tenderness toward you. His love is relational: "*I have loved you … with an everlasting love. With unfailing love I have drawn you to myself*" (Jeremiah 31:3b).

Even if you've felt separated from Him and haven't abided in His presence, He knows your history. He pursues you, like David writes: "*Your beauty and love chase me every day of my life*" (Psalm 23:6, MSG). A pursuit is a quest, a search, or to be trailing behind someone. God is always right there, ready to pour out goodness onto you. His delight is in His love for you.

I grew up being dropped off at different churches, as at that time my parents didn't regularly attend anywhere. I knew of God and was told that Jesus loved me, and I enjoyed going to Sunday school and kids' clubs. Though I never fully understood salvation or scripture, God had chosen me. In His choosing, He was going to pursue me and keep calling me to Him. As a teenager, I experienced moments of encounter with Him. I remember attending a party at a stranger's house. Halfway through the evening, I felt a stirring inside, telling me that something wasn't right and to leave the house. I knew it was God. To this day I don't know why He prompted me to leave, but I knew at the time I was hearing from a higher power.

He pursued me even in my rejection of Him. It wasn't until I was in my early twenties that I gave my life fully over to Him. This pursuit is a natural outpouring of His affection for us. He passionately desires a relationship with us and keeps giving gifts of His attention to let us know He's truly there. When you look back on your life, can you see His fingerprints? Are there moments in your own rejection of Him that you experienced Him chasing after you, showering you with His thoughtfulness? He will never fade away, and He will never turn His back on you. You are His child, and He gifts you all the fullness of His devotion.

I received my first prophetic word spoken over me during a ladies' morning at church. One of the pastors came in to pray over the women's group. I was a newer Christian at that point. I remember the pastor coming toward me, and with the whole group observing, speaking over me. It was a surreal experience, as if someone had gotten inside my brain and was splitting open all my baggage for all to see. He said, "There have been lies spoken over you. The same lies repeatedly. God says that what they said about you is not true; that's not how He sees you. He loves you and He says to let those lies go now. He has made you a warrior for Him."

I was in shock. How did this man know about what had been said to me? I had been living with an inner sense of unworthiness and filled with self-deprecating thoughts. As a child I was told I wasn't wanted, and that life would be easier without me. As a broken teenager, I made choices that led to mounting shame and regret, which turned into gossip and a soured reputation. My eating disorder told me that I wasn't worthy until I reached perfection. How could this stranger pierce my heart like this?

After that experience, I was convinced that God saw me that day. That He noticed me. It wasn't until I learned about fullness that I realized He saw me every day. God knows everything that you think nobody knows about. His devotion to you, His daughter, means that He never lets you out of His sight. As you let Him in deeper and believe that He has time for you, you will experience for yourself His steadfastness. In Psalm 149:4, the psalmist talks about how the Lord delights in His people. You are His people, and He finds joy in knowing everything about you. You are the only one of you that He created, and He pays special attention to you because you matter to Him.

In this fullness of love, we have the privilege to live before His throne. Jesus lives in us, the Holy Spirit empowers us, and God our Father and King takes care of us:

> *And so, dear brothers and sisters, we can boldly enter heaven's Most Holy Place because of the blood of Jesus. By his death, Jesus opened a new and life-giving way through the curtain into the Most Holy Place. And since we have a great High Priest who rules over God's house, let us go right into the presence of God with sincere hearts fully trusting him. For our guilty consciences have been sprinkled with Christ's blood to make us clean, and our bodies have been washed with pure water.* (Hebrews 10:19–22)

This was God's dream all along, ever since the fall of man in the garden. He wanted to cleanse us and make a way for us to approach Him again. He sent Jesus so that His dream could be a reality. Sin had come into the world and destroyed His opportunity to have a relationship with you. The garden was taken away, and the time of wandering began. Through His blood, Jesus atoned for all that aimless roaming, and you can now step past the thicket and into the garden again. He is so excited to have you back. Let him tend to you. He will never leave you. He has promised to be with you to the end of the world and then face-to-face in Heaven: "'For I know the plans I have for you,' declares the Lord, 'plans to prosper you and not to harm you, plans to give you hope and a future,'" (Jeremiah 29:11, NIV). A future speaks of what's ahead, what is still to come. He declares that He knows it all, resides over your future, and has good plans for you.

A few months after I gave my life to Christ, someone vandalized my car tire outside of my apartment building. I wasn't married yet, and I was working a lower wage job to pay my rent and vehicle insurance, without extras to cover new tires. My boyfriend, who is now my husband, came to my apartment one day with a cheque, relaying that his aunt, who at that point I didn't know very well, had given him the money. She had told him that God had told her to write a cheque for a certain amount and give it to us. I opened the cheque and, to my disbelief, the amount was within one dollar of what I'd been quoted to replace the tire. God knew me and saw me. He wasn't going anywhere, and He wanted me to know that He was looking after me.

God assures us that He never changes: "*Whatever is good and perfect is a gift coming down to us from God our Father, who created all the lights in the heavens. He never changes or casts a shifting shadow*" (James 1:17). He wants to gift us with provision and small tokens of His affection. Think of the times you prayed for something and it was answered exactly as you requested, or when you were surprised by something someone said that spoke directly to your heart. In those moments, He is saying, "I love you and I'll never leave you." I underlined a passage in Psalms in my Bible that speaks of how our Father God watches us from Heaven: "*The Lord looks down from Heaven and sees the whole human race. From his throne he observes all who live on Earth. He made their hearts, so he understands everything they do*" (Psalm 33:13–15).

There is no moment in your life, past, present, or future, when He withdrew His attention and affection from you.

In your relationship with Father God, He wakes with you and goes to sleep with you. He travels with you and plans with you. He is fully committed to you.

As part of the fullness of His devotion for you, He will surround and defend you: "*God has made everything beautiful for its own time. He has planted eternity in the human heart, but even so people cannot see the whole scope of God's work from beginning to end*" (Ecclesiastes 3:11). We often hear about believers who feel abandoned by God in their moment of weakness or their trial. They say that they don't know where God is, and they can't see Him working. Within the promise of salvation is the assurance that He is the sovereign king who brings all things to justice. When you can't see or feel Him, you can rest in the promise that His Word says that He watches you from Heaven. He is working it out, and in your fullness of rest you can trust Him to take care of you. He is able to restore and rebuild.

We can't see the whole picture that God can. We can feel helpless at times, desperate even, in our lack of control. God says, "Although you see in part, I see it all. I know how you're struggling, and I commit at all times to stay at your side through this. You can't see what I can see right now. Rest in me and accept my promise to always work on your behalf."

Now we see things imperfectly, like puzzling reflections in a mirror, but then we will see everything with perfect clarity. All I know now is partial and incomplete, but then I will know everything completely, just as God now knows me completely. (1 Corinthians 13:12)

Christ blesses us in our humanness and never condemns us for being flesh. He gifts us His devotion because He understands that we need His undivided attention in our frailness to rise above the evil in the world: "*Because of our faith, Christ has brought us into this place of undeserved privilege where we now stand, and we confidently and joyfully look forward to sharing God's glory*" (Romans 5:2).

In our standing within undeserved privilege, we own our birthright inside the kingdom family. We are God's children, and we have rights within that placement. We have the right to protection from our Father God, the right to peace, and the right to unconditional hope. Paul speaks of this hope and joy within our birthright:

Now may God, the inspiration and fountain of hope, fill you to overflowing with uncontainable joy and perfect peace as you trust in him. And may the power of the Holy Spirit continually surround your life with his super-abundance until you radiate with hope! (Romans 15:13, TPT)

He promises to be your hope and fill you with joy and peace, simply because you chose to trust in Him. Through faith, these aren't possibilities—these are assurances. Take hold of what belongs to you. Joy and peace are yours in Him.

Throughout this process to find fullness, I was often sidetracked, wondering why God would be so good to me. Shame can erode the confidence in our hearts that tells us we are worthy of such love and affection. Emotional wounds can deceive us into believing that no one is purely good, solidifying a general distrust of humanity. But our God is innately good, and He has the power to renew your mind and rebuild your self-worth. God understands that we've gone through trials; He knows that the fall of the world has caused every one of His beloved creations to believe lies about themselves and distort the truth about love. In fullness, God asks you to let Him be good to you now. He desires to teach you what a first-class father is like. He craves to pour into your identity and bring you to the full realization that you are His priority. The whole picture, the garden, the seed called Jesus—it was all for you.

It took some time for me to feel like our new home was home. Many nights I tried to sleep, with the moon shining through my window, but I felt lonely. I knew I wasn't alone, but my home had changed, and it felt peculiar. I prayed every day for the house to feel like home. One morning I walked into my new closet and felt an overwhelming sense of God's presence and adoration for me. This was personal for me, and exactly how God blesses us. He knew that the place to pour His affection on me in our new house would be inside my closet. Fashion is a source of fun for me, and my closet was one of my favourite treats inside our new house, with its shelves and hooks for organizing all my items. It was a space I felt was truly my own within a family of five. I once again realized His specific care over me. He was there with me, inside this new house. He had always been my home.

> *Those who live in the shelter of the Most High will find rest in the shadow of the Almighty. This I declare about the Lord: He alone is my refuge, my place of safety; he is my God, and I trust him.* (Psalm 91:1–2)

God offers us this comfortable position in Him, one that never changes and that resides in us wherever we go. Lean into the home He gifts you, the home of a loving and gentle Father who lives to love you. Love Him in return with all the praise and thanksgiving He deserves. Let Him fully in, unreserved and defenceless. Allow Him to see your weakness, your brittle humanness. He is beckoning you to walk with Him into the garden again. It's a tender journey with no timeline, as He is with you forever. If you run away, He will find you and bring you back home in Him. It's a relentless pursuit.

In Philippians 2:1–17, Paul teaches us how to flourish within the fullness of God. This is the fruit of blossoming in Him. When we release our control and tell God He can take us where He wants to, we become more full in Him. It implores us to stay tender-hearted and compassionate, like our Saviour. It speaks of agreeing with one another and working together with one mind and purpose, to be the light of the world, sharing our stories and letting ourselves be seen. Paul encourages us to shine brightly for Christ, to show the results of our salvation, to obey God with deep reverence, and live what the Bible teaches. It promises that God is working in you, giving you the desire and the power to do what pleases Him. That's the power of Him.

Jesus's very first miracle was to make something empty full again, as described in John's account of the wedding at Cana (John 2:1–11). Big stone jars were sitting empty, needing to be filled again for the celebration to continue. Father God uses this scene to unleash the first revelation of His power and plan. Don't miss the significance here. The jars were empty, and the miracle was that He made them full again. A miraculous display of fullness was first on the list!

What Christ is doing in you has never been done before, because there is only one you. Living within fullness, your uniqueness of character and how God has gifted you means that your story will be its own. Your life isn't going to look like anyone else's. In fullness, your one-of-a-kind self becomes the instrument of God's love. Psalm 148 declares that everything that God created praises Him—the oceans, the creatures within them, the mountains, and the skies. These things praise Him simply by being what they were created to be. You praise Him by being you. Unequivocally and uniquely you. The only one there is. Your every breath brings Him praise because He loves you.

In 1 Timothy 6:6, Paul says, "*Yet true godliness with contentment is itself great wealth.*" The world says to leave your mark, make a name for yourself, and you'll find contentment. Christ says, "I made the world; I am the mark. I died to gift you contentment, and it's yours to hold. Let my devotion to you be a sweet song over your life. Rest in me, let me heal and lead you now. Together we will advance my kingdom."

Look at yourself in the mirror. Look into your eyes. Imagine looking at your reflection and feeling complete freedom to be yourself. Imagine a life where you had no obligations and the world didn't set the bar. Let expectations and pressure fade with the knowledge of His passion for you. Believe that your whole life is a love story of your rescue and restoration. You were never meant to wander until Heaven. He is stretching out His hand. Will you take it?

It's springtime as I write this. Small buds have appeared on each of our freshly planted trees. I can't wait to see their blossoms in a few weeks. Looking at my trees, I think of fullness. Every time we step into a place of fullness in Christ and welcome Him in, our leaves sprout a little bigger. He is our gardener. He knows exactly what we need to flourish in how He has created us. What a beautiful gift, the fullness of life. We were meant to bloom.

When I think of all this, I fall to my knees and pray to the Father, the Creator of everything in heaven and on earth. I pray that from his glorious, unlimited resources he will empower you with inner strength through his Spirit. Then Christ will make his home in your hearts as you trust in him. Your roots will grow down into God's love and keep you strong. And may you have all the power to understand, as all God's people should, how wide, how long, how high, and how deep his love is. May you experience the love of Christ, though it is too great to understand fully. Then you will be made complete with all the fullness of life and power that comes from God. Now all glory to God, who is able, through his mighty power at work within us, to accomplish infinitely more than we might ask or think. Glory to him in the church and in Christ Jesus through all generations forever and ever! Amen. (Ephesians 3:14–21)

REMEMBER THE GIFT: TIME

Time is God's devotion to you. He is your Creator, and He lives to pour His tenderness and love over you every moment of your day. Time says that the whole plan was for you. This life is your love story with Him. He delights in your every moment. He holds your future. Time means that He will never let go of you.

PLANT THE SEED

1. When you think about God's gift of time, what excites you the most? How does His gift of complete devotion to you change the way you think of Him? Tell God what His devotion to you means to your heart and thank Him for His pure love over you.

_____

_____

_____

_____

_____

2. Have you accepted each gift of fullness? Take some time to meditate on the essence of God and what the fullness of life means for you in the here and now. How would accepting the fullness transform who you are and the way you release yourself? God wants you to bloom in His fullness. Tell God you're ready to blossom in the wake of His love.

_____

_____

_____

_____

_____

Blossom Prayer

Lord, help me to comprehend and accept this deep love you have over me. I'm so grateful that nothing separates us. You're such a good and loving Father. Remind me of your devotion to me on the days I wander from you or doubt my worth. Thank you for the moments in my life when you pursued me in my rejection. Help me to devote myself to you like you devote yourself to me. I praise you for how you love me. Increase my trust in the fact that you hold my future, and your plans are always good. Tear down the pride that keeps me from accepting your full devotion to me. Lord, now that I know and understand the fullness of life, I want to bloom in you. God, I relent my control and I ask that you come now and release me into my true self, the one you decided on and created. Give me eyes to see myself as you see me. Come into every crack of

my soul and tend to me like a garden you cherish. I trust you, Father. I love you so much, God. Thank you for this gift. Amen.

A Letter from the Father

Dear Daughter,

My child, you are my girl. My beloved. You are beautiful and elegant, and I love everything about how I created you. I especially enjoy seeing you smile, and my heart fills when you laugh. I love the moments when you're unafraid and carefree. That's how I see you even when you don't. My eyes see your freedom in me. Walk with me into that freedom now, daughter. Deeper still. I'm reaching out my hand to you. Your freedom is more than a passing thought, an idea, or fleeting moment. Your freedom is in who I am for you. I am everything. I am your peace. I am your joy. I am your provision. I give you living water to drink from daily. The water I give to you replenishes the weight that the world drains from you and refreshes your mind so that you can find joy again. Let me in deeper. I want you to know more of my heart for you. Do you not know how much I love you, daughter? My heart aches with deep, sincere adoration when I think of you. I know the intricate pieces of you. I formed the depths of your soul. In me, you find your strength and portion. In me, your Father, you are whole. Look to me when you find yourself fading again. I can always see you, the real you. Your identity rests in who I say you are. You wear the royal clothing of righteousness in which I have dressed you. You carry kindness, patience, forgiveness, compassion, quiet strength, humility, and discipline every minute of your day. Never forget that your brother came and took your heaviness from you. You are healed in His name. You are a member of my kingdom family, and your inheritance is yours to take hold of. You stand in a new placement now. Royalty. A daughter of the highest king. My princess. You are so valuable to me. Daughter, let's always be close. I want you to know my character and understand my devotion to you. Stay with me. Walk with me. In me, you are the true you. In our intimacy, you find your freedom. The freedom to be you. Absolutely, incredibly you. My special one. The only one of you there is. I'm so glad you're you. I wouldn't change a thing about you. I created you because I loved the thought of you, and I knew the world would be a better place with you in it. Believe with me that you are enough. Oh, and remember, I'm always here with you. Even if you don't feel me, I am right here. It's a promise, and I never break my promises to you.

I love you, precious girl.
Your Heavenly Dad

Scriptures to Counter Striving

TO COUNTER STRIVING FOR RECOGNITION

"Jesus told them, 'This is the only work God wants from you: Believe in the one he has sent'" (John 6:29).

"So humble yourselves under the mighty power of God, and at the right time he will lift you up in honor" (1 Peter 5:6).

"Do not love this world nor the things it offers you, for when you love the world, you do not have the love of the Father in you" (1 John 2:15).

"And this world is fading away, along with everything that people crave. But anyone who does what pleases God will live forever" (1 John 2:17).

"Work with enthusiasm, as though you were working for the Lord rather than for people" (Ephesians 6:7).

"God paid a high price for you, so don't be enslaved by the world" (1 Corinthians 7:23).

"The Lord replied, 'I will personally go with you, Moses, and I will give you rest …'" (Exodus 33:14a).

TO COUNTER COMPARISON AND STRIVING FOR PERFECTION

"*For the wisdom of this world is foolishness to God. As the Scriptures say, 'He traps the wise in the snare of their own cleverness'*" (1 Corinthians 3:19).

"*There are different kinds of service, but we serve the same Lord. God works in different ways, but it is the same God who does the work in all of us*" (1 Corinthians 12:5–6).

"*Those of you who use the things of the world should not become attached to them. For this world as we know it will soon pass away*" (1 Corinthians 7:31).

"*So let's stop condemning each other. Decide instead to live in such a way that you will not cause another believer to stumble and fall*" (Romans 14:13).

"*After starting your new lives in the Spirit, why are you now trying to become perfect by your own human effort?*" (Galatians 3:3b).

"*But the Holy Spirit produces this kind of fruit in our lives: love, joy, peace, patience, kindness, goodness, faithfulness, gentleness, and self-control*" (Galatians 5:22–23a).

TO COUNTER STRIVING FOR BELONGING

"*See how much our Father loves us, for he calls us his children, and that is what we are!*" (1 John 3:1a).

"*But you belong to God, my dear children. you have already won a victory ... because the Spirit who lives in you is greater than the spirit who lives in the world*" (1 John 4:4).

"*For God knew his people in advance, and he chose them to become like his Son, so that his Son would be the firstborn amount many brothers and sisters*" (Romans 8:29).

"*For his Spirit joins with our spirit to affirm that we are God's children*" (Romans 8:16).

"*And because you belong to him, the power of the life-giving Spirit has freed you from the power of sin that leads to death*" (Romans 8:2).

The Meeting Place

INSPIRED BY PSALM 91

*I enter the throne room of my Father God
and I see Him there,
like a shining light,
like a gentle spirit with forging strength.
It's Him. It's really Him.
Kneeling down before Him, I am overwhelmed with
feelings of His love washing over me.
He cups my chin and lifts my eyes up to His face and
tells me He is glad to see me here again. He tells me
my prayers are important to Him, and what matters to
me matters to Him too.
I lay my head on top of his knees and feel peace.
It's so good to be with Him.
Sitting here, I can't remember
why I came to Him again,
I can only feel fullness.
Then I see them, the prayers I brought to Him today,
filling up a bowl beside Him,
and He tells me the requests are safe
within His control.
I don't want to leave the throne room,
leave His presence,
but the daily grind is calling me back.
I tell Him I will be back soon, and He says,
"I know, dear. I can't wait."*

*I ask Him if I am going to be okay today, even with
everything that I am burdened by,
and He tells me to release myself,
to let go and let Him take the lead.
He reminds me of who I am in Him.
"You are my daughter, don't forget. Everything my Son
Jesus has is yours too. We are a
family. There is no reason to fear the world or what's to
come, because I have promised you
that I am taking care of everything. This feeling that
you have here in this room with Me,
take it with you. Everywhere you go, take Me with you.
I am your Father, and I protect you
and lead you. I provide all that your heart needs, even
when you don't realize what you're aching for. Precious
girl, I love you so much. You got this in Me."
So I leave the room. Turning back, I see Him smile and
nod and cover His chest with His hand.
"I'm in here," He says to me.
Leaving the throne, I face my day, knowing that I am
enough, because He says I am.*